Grimoire Dehara

Book Two: Ulani

Grimoire Dehara
Book Two: Ulani

Storm Constantine & Taylor Ellwood

Megalithica Books
Stafford England

Grimoire Dehara Book Two: Ulani
By Storm Constantine & Taylor Ellwood © 2016

Cover Design: Ruby
Interior Illustrations: All by Ruby, but for those on the following pages, which are by Storm Constantine: 23, 30, 36, 40, 60, 70, 176, 179
Interior Design: Storm Constantine

Set in Book Antiqua

MB0184

ISBN: 978-0-9932371-8-8 (paperback edition)

A Megalithica Books edition
An imprint of Immanion Press Edition
http://www.immanion-press.com
info@immanion-press.com

Contents

Preface by Storm Constantine   9
Foreword by Taylor Ellwood   13

Acantha
The Tiers and Castes of Dehara   16
The Meaning of Ulani   17
The Path of the Acanthalid   18
The Symbol Acantha   19
Meditation upon Acantha   20
The Spiral Gate   20
A Rehuna's Experience of Acantha   21
Acantha Ascension
Invocation of the Aurago   25
The Breath of Lusteration   26
The Breath of Transformation   27
Summoning the Aurago   27
Ascension Majhahn   28
Working Within the Ethers
The Etheric Nayati   31
Expanding the Etheric Nayati   32
Etheric Realms   33
Aganymphna: the Sacred Flower   33
The Garden of Night   35
Aloyt: Dehar of Dreams
The Aloytic Realm   39
Sikaara
The Energy System of the Body   43
The Correspondences of the Sikras   44
Sikaara Meditations   50
Dehara Demitto of Acantha
Abrimel   57
Characteristics of Abrimel   58
Xynlis the Gatekeeper   59
The Cloister of Abrimel Majhahn   61

Pyralis
The Path of the Pyralisit   67
The Symbol Pyralis   68
Meditation Upon Pyralis   69

Revisiting the Dehara   71
Purging by Fire
   Majhahns to Deal with Conflict, Pain and Justice   75
   Majhahn of Forgiveness and Banishment   76
   Variations on the Majhahn of Forgiveness   79
   The Mahallatu: Dark Riders of Justice   80
   Agave Majhahn of Justice   86
Alchemical Transformation   89
   The Dehara of Alchemy   90
      Areha   91
      Elolis   92
      Lhah   93
      Voorhalis   94
      Dvelin   95
      Baloor   96
      Phynix   97
   The Stages of Transformation
      Calcination   98
      Dissolution   99
      Separation   101
      Conjunction   102
      Fermentation   104
      Distillation   105
      Coagulation   106
Pyralis Ascension
   Xephelax: The Dark Labyrinth   107
   Ponclast: Dehar Demitto of Xephelax   107
   Sikaara Work with Xephelax: Va-Sikra   110
   Descent into Xephelax   111
   One: The Road to Xephelax, the Gate of Mal
   & the Chamber of Aurith   113
   Two: The Chamber of Saal   117
   Three: The Chamber of Alik   119
   Four: The Chamber of Azul   121
   Five: The Chamber of Iskara   123
   Six: The Chamber of Malith   125
   Seven: The Heart of Xephelax   127

Algoma
   The Path of the Algomalid   131
   The Symbol Algoma   132
   Meditation Upon Algoma   133

The Blossoming Light	134
Merging With the Dehara	135
Merging with Miyacala	137
Merging with Agave	141
Merging with Lunil	145
Merging with Aruhani	149
Guides and Companions	
Mair Vayairh the Golden-Eyed	153
Harrahn, Dehar of Restfulness	156
The Hienamas of the Tribes	157
Primordial Tribes	158
Uigenna	161
Unneah	163
Varr	165
Sulh	167
Kakkahaar	169
Colurastes	171
Sarock	173
Gelaming	175
Divozenky – Mind of the Earth	177
A Visit to Helek Sah and the Mind of Divozenky	180
Constellati – The Walkers Between the Stars	187
Astraclaustri: Gatekeeper of the Cosmos	188
The Spiritual Pearl	
Algoma Ascension Majhahn	191
Pearl Breathing	192
Moving Essence into the Spiritual Pearl	193
Empowerment of Earth and Stars	194
The Majhahn of Emergence	195
Thiede's Domain	197
The Role of the Hienama	201
Appendices	
The Wraeththu Mythos	204
Ascension Majhahns	211
Further Tribes of Wraeththu	214
Resources	217
Glossary	218

Acknowledgements

Thanks must go to everyone who has worked on and in the dehara system since its inception ten years ago.

Daniel Marcheschi for initiating and running the Nayati Dehara group online, whose members kindly shared their magical and spiritual experiences, which contributed greatly to this book.

Daniela Ritter, who is a member of Nayati Dehara, through which she contributed ideas for the Deharan system's development, and who is also a writer within the Wraeththu Mythos.

Ellen and Paul Kesterton, who worked with us on the original Kaimana material and who also contributed to more recent work on Dehara.

Ruby for her fantastic illustrations for this grimoire, and all the other beautiful Wraeththu pictures she has provided over the years.

Preface
by Storm Constantine

I began writing about Wraeththu in my teens, when I first discovered books on magic and alchemy. I deplored the way humanity was rapaciously destroying its home – the earth – and, with youthful idealism, dreamed of a superior race coming to replace it, a species that was connected with the natural world, not estranged from it. Wraeththu are androgynous beings, the genders no longer split into two but both aspects existing comfortably within each individual. The idea for them was partly inspired by the alchemical rebis – the divine hermaphrodite, the fruit of the sacred marriage, or chymical wedding. Otherwise known as the *hieros gamos* within alchemical lore, this 'marriage' was the union of opposites, a god and goddess, resulting in the perfect form of the rebis, a reconciliation of matter and spirit. I've often utilised alchemical symbols and ideas in my fiction, and especially so in the Wraeththu Mythos.

In my imagined world, I saw the earth itself as an intelligent entity. These early Gaian tendencies, melded with my interest in the rebis and alchemy, eventually formed the foundation of what became the lore of the Wraeththu Mythos.

When, in my twenties, I began to write more seriously about hara (as Wraeththu are termed), I found them not to be perfect, but struggling to overcome and transcend the human traits within them, to fulfil their potential as inheritors of the earth.

But perhaps their failings were partly what made them so endearing to readers – the books claimed a loyal following, which has persisted to this day.

I wrote the first three Wraeththu novels in the 1980s but, after the millennium, returned to their world for a new series of books, which has since been followed by another trilogy and four shared world anthologies, written with other authors. Over the years, the mythos attracted a loyal following of fans, many of whom empathised with, or were interested in, the magic used by Wraeththu in the novels. I thought it would be interesting to expand the ideas within the fiction and create a rounded system of Wraeththu magic. Certain characters within the mythos had become iconic – archetypes even – and were ideal for incorporation within a magical system such as Dehara.

The creation of magical systems, especially when based on cultural or fictional ideas, can properly be defined as Pop Culture Magic. Pop Culture magicians perceive the possibility of magic in every walk of life and acknowledge the fact that icons of our culture can be viewed and used as magical entities.

The initial focus of a magical system is the entities and deities around which the system revolves. The gods of Wraeththu are called dehara (day-hara), singular dehar (day-har). They came to me as I was writing the fiction, presenting themselves to my imagination, often in astoundingly vivid forms, and are the foundation of this system of magic.

Gods and goddesses can be seen frequencies of the universal life force. The faces given to them are merely masks that enable people to interact with formless energy. Humans work better with pictures than abstract ideas. Also, when a great many people invest energy into something – in the form of thought, intention and emotion – it is fed by that energy and acquires a vicarious independent existence. What vitalises all the religions and magical systems of the world? Human thought, human emotion, human will and human intention. The stuff of creation can be seen as a kind of modelling clay. It can be moulded into certain shapes, with certain attributes.

One of the ways in which this system was developed was

through visionary questing, whereby the practitioner projects their mind into a visualised environment, then wanders through it, noting what they see and hear. This technique has been used (and still is) to quest for information about the Wraeththu gods, the dehara. Through this interaction, the system is as limitless as the imaginations of those involved in it. From a Pop Culture Magic point of view, practitioners are quite capable of creating new systems, thought forms and deities, which have as much relevance as existing systems, and are often more dynamic.

Although magic can be used to affect reality, in the form of rituals to achieve a desired effect, the individual practitioner can also use it as a tool for self-development. In the ancient system of alchemy, alchemists were said to be looking for the means to transform base metal into gold. While this might well have had a literal meaning, it's commonly accepted that this was also a metaphor for spiritual enlightenment, the quest for true awareness and self-knowledge. The gold in question was that of the spirit, and all the different processes of the alchemical transformation applied to the being of the alchemist.

As part of our research, my colleague, Taylor Ellwood, and I have explored the ideas and models used in other systems, such as meditation, breathing techniques, spiritual healing, the energy system of the body, chakra work and so on. Such practices are the backbone of self-advancement techniques but in order to incorporate them into Dehara, they needed to have the right 'flavour' – hence the reimagining. We do not intend to present any of these techniques as 'new' – they are tried and tested, in some cases for centuries – but as traditional practices with a Deharan slant.

As with any magical tradition, Deharan Magic can be used to affect reality, in the form of majhahns (rituals) to achieve a specific effect, and to facilitate self-evolution through meditation and majhahn. We make no claims that Dehara is better than any other system; it is just different.

Another point I feel obliged to cover is that we are not, through publishing this system, attempting to create a religion. To us, magic and religion are separate. This is magic. If used

11

properly it can be a tool for self-progression, but that is down to the individual.

When I first began writing about Wraeththu, way back in the 1970s, many aspects of sexuality and gender were still taboo and not discussed openly – such as transgender and intersex people. I created my fictional race ignorant of what has now become gender awareness and the politics that accompany it. I used the pronoun 'he' to describe hara. This is probably an unconscious sign of the era into which I was born and brought up. In a sense, those early novels have become historical documents. Within Deharan magic, the masculine pronoun can be replaced with one of the practitioner's choosing where applicable within the majhahns.

This is the second volume in a three book series. Each volume focuses upon one tier of the magical system. Book One, *Grimoire Dehara: Kaimana*, was published by Immanion Press over ten years ago, and it's taken this long for Taylor and I to find the time to expand the system with book two, *Grimoire Dehara: Ulani*. We are working on the third book, *Grimoire Dehara: Nahir Nuri*, simultaneously, and intend to leave no more than a year or so's gap between this volume and the final book.

While experienced practitioners of magic will hopefully find this material interesting, it's preferable for anyone intending to work with the ideas in this book to have had experience of the first tier, Kaimana, first. Otherwise, you will come to the system one third of the way through it. For the purposes of continuity, the introductory material from Kaimana, which describes the world of Wraeththu and its mythos, are included for reference in the appendices of this volume, but the actual work of the first tier appears in the initial grimoire.

Storm Constantine
July 2016

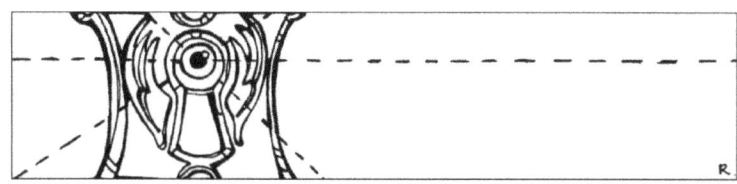

Foreword
by Taylor Ellwood

Just over a decade ago, Storm Constantine wrote and published *Grimoire Dehara: Kaimana*. For approximately two years before that Storm, myself, and a few other people had been putting together the Dehara system and experimenting with it. When the first grimoire came out, readers of the *Wraeththu* series were excited because here finally was a system of magic based around the series. Now eleven years later *Grimoire Dehara: Ulani* is at last coming out.

Approximately a year ago, Storm asked if I would co-write and develop *Grimoire Dehara: Ulani* with her. At the time I was writing *Pop Culture Magic 2.0*, so it seemed appropriate that I work on a pop culture magic system. And the time was right, because both Storm and I had a decade of experiences and work with the Dehara system to inform not only the writing of *Ulani* but the sequel after it.

Right before Storm and I started writing this book, I reread the entire *Wraeththu* series. I hadn't read the series for a long time and it was wonderful to reacquaint myself with the beloved characters of the series, to reconnect fully with the magic of the books. The *Wraeththu* series played a significant role in inspiring my approach to pop culture magic in general, and of course to the work we've done with the *Dehara* series.

What you have in your hands is the next level of the Dehara system, and an invitation to further explore the wonders of Wraeththu. I hope you'll join in the work to continue manifesting this pop culture magic system into the world.

Taylor Ellwood
Mad Scientist and Magical Experimenter
Portland, Oregon
May 2016

The Tiers and Castes of Dehara

KAIMANA 'The Path of the Seeker'

1: Ara - altar
2: Neoma - new moon
3: Brynie – strong

ULANI 'The Path to the Cosmos'

1: Acantha - thorns
2: Pyralis – fire
3: Algoma - valley of flowers

NAHIR-NURI 'The Path of the Infinite'

1: Efrata – distinguished
2: Aislinn - vision
3: Cleatha - glory

Acantha

The Meaning of Ulani

The first tier of learning within the Deharan system is Kaimana, which means 'the Path of the Seeker'. It encompasses the initial levels of learning – including the discovery of the dehara and working with them, as well as encouragement of a connection with the earth through the observance of the natural seasons of the year.

Ulani was originally named 'the Path of the Cosmos', but should be more properly termed 'the Path *to* the Cosmos'. This is because the Ulani tier's focus is still mainly upon the earthly realm, even though it leads eventually to Nahir Nuri, the third tier, which is 'the Path of the Infinite'. The aim of Ulani is work on the self, for the rehuna to explore their psyches, overcome inner demons and build strength on all levels of being. At its latter stages, in the Algoma caste, Ulani augments the rehuna's connection with the earth and leads at last to the cosmic realms. But what takes place in Ulani is only a visit to the threshold. True exploration of the ethers and cosmic realms takes place in Nahir Nuri training.

The Path of the Acanthalid

Here now, between the high mountains, follow the path of thorns to further knowledge...

Within the Deharan system, Ulani, the second tier, represents greater knowledge and understanding. It is the journeyman stage of progression. The rehuna now has the means to affect reality and the symbols of the three levels can be used actively in magical work.

The meaning of Acantha is 'thorns'. After the realisation of Brynie and the completion of Kaimana, the rehuna must look inward. The rehuna now considers they are the sum of their life experiences, in all of their glory and terror.

Acantha is thorny – it is the dark night of the soul, the facing of inner demons and awareness and acceptance of all personal traits. The rehuna now enters the shadow world. They face the darkness within and without. Only then can they progress to Pyralis, the way of fire.

Acantha is the way of the self. Only by knowing themselves thoroughly may the rehuna progress upon the path of knowledge. Acantha offers the opportunity of freedom from delusion and self-deceit.

As with the techniques given in the previous tier, the rehuna should visualise themselves during majhahn as having an androgynous form – a magical identity different from their everyday self.

The Symbol Acantha

The fourth caste symbol in the Deharan system represents knowledge that becomes power that becomes knowledge... essentially a cycle. It reminds us that an ending is a beginning and a beginning is an ending. It is the power of transition, the importance of flow and change, adaptability. Part of being able to change reality is to recognise that there are no patterns, that in fact we make the patterns and create reality.

One of the functions of the symbol of Acantha is to help the rehuna delve deeper into the etheric realms. It is, like Ara, a portal, but to areas of higher vibration.

Acantha is limitless potential and can be used in majhahn to help manifest goals. It represents the rehuna's willingness to open themselves to deeper experience, to tread more difficult paths in the search for knowledge and evolution.

Acantha is drawn by beginning at the foot and working up to and through the triple spiral. The horizontal line is added last. The symbol may be visualised as three dimensional, with the tail being closer than the spiral, and the bar passing through the loop and then through the heart of the spiral.

Meditation upon Acantha

'My Nayati is a room at the top of a nine-sided tower. There are tall arched windows in the facets of the walls. Each of these windows is a gateway to the realm of one of the tiers of Deharan magic. The windows may be curtained or left open to the sky. When I focus upon a particular symbol, I will drape all the other windows, leaving one clear. I perform my meditations upon the symbols at dusk or dawn, when the light is changing.'

Before embarking upon any other work for the caste of Acantha, the rehuna should spend at least one session contemplating the symbol and its associations. The rehuna, being by now fully experienced in the practices associated with Kaimana, may devise their own meditation for this purpose. The example given below is a suggestion for how to interact with the symbol.

The Spiral Gate

The rehuna should prepare for meditation in their customary manner and evoke around themselves their etheric Nayati.

Visualise the symbol Acantha before you, either as being an object within your Nayati or in the air before you.

For some minutes contemplate the symbol, examine it and see what ideas might come to you. Note what colour it appears to you. Or perhaps its colour shifts as you focus your attention upon it.

Then make the symbol increase in size until it is at least the same size as you. Focus upon its aspect as a gateway. This could appear as a glowing portal hanging before you, or a symbol on the ground, painted, or made of sand, stone, or crystals.

Pass through the gateway, either by walking through the symbol if it hangs before you, or else by walking its path as if it is inscribed on the ground. Pass into whatever realm lies beyond and explore.

When you are ready to return to normal consciousness, complete the meditation in your usual manner.

A Rehuna's Experience of Acantha

To me, Acantha was 'the road through the wall'. When I first began working on it some years ago, I felt that the territory I'd find beyond the wall would be totally new and unknown. I'd had some interesting experiences working through Kaimana, with visualisations becoming ever more 'spacy'. I was meeting entities I termed the 'Star Walkers', particularly when doing the Chamber of Gateways meditation.

For me personally – and this does not necessarily mean it's the path for all rehunas – the different tiers appear to lead inevitably into the ethers, to space/time magic. However, I also felt that the true experience of this kind of work is really the province of Nahir Nuri, so I regard Ulani as a grounding after perhaps rarefied experiences at the conclusion of Brynie.

With this in mind, I began to look upon Acantha – whose name means 'thorny' after all – as a means to work upon self-awareness, self-knowledge, as well as a framework upon which to stretch my magical wings. So the road through the wall did not lead to cosmic landscapes as I'd once expected, but rather a grassy, wooded hill at sunset. The idea of descending the hill, into whatever communities lay below, seemed a metaphor for looking inward, for honing skills and hands-on work, rather than dreaming among the stars.

Acantha did bring some very thorny issues to the fore in my life that had to be dealt with. At the time, it seriously affected

21

my faith in myself and my ability to effect change, but in retrospect I can see all that happened for the lesson it was. I had to assimilate certain lessons before I could move on, but that is not solely the province of magic. It is part of life, whether you are spiritually/magically inclined or not. A more spiritual individual will obviously experience these life lessons in a different way to someone who lives entirely in the material world. And I think, for this reason, sometimes the lessons are somewhat sharper for the rehuna (or any practitioner of magic) – thorn in the flesh, remember? A forest of thorns, as in fairy tales, could be good imagery to work with during Acantha.

In undertaking any kind of magical/spiritual path with seriousness, you are dedicating yourself to evolving the self, and often it feels like the more knowledge you gain, the less you know. This is another aspect of Acantha.

Acantha Ascension

Invocation of the Aurago

The aurago, personal to the rehuna, is the representation of their innermost wisdom, a guide into the deeper mysteries of their calling. It is an attendant spirit, a genius, (in the sense of a guiding spirit or tutelary deity), and while not a dehar, may be represented by a deified hero or fictional character.

In order for the rehuna to ascend from Brynie to Acantha, and into Ulani, they should undertake an initiation to meet their personal aurago. This entity isn't a dehar, but a being of energy. It might appear to the rehuna as another har, or as a supernatural entity, or a character from Wraeththu lore, depending on the individual. The aurago is separate to the hienama entity invoked by the rehuna during Kaimana training, and is associated with higher levels of learning and experience. The aurago initiation raises the rehuna from one level to another by virtue of the path the aurago sets them upon.

To perform this initiation, the rehuna should enter into a deep meditative state, through breathing techniques that will prepare their internal energy for connection with the aurago. There are two specific breathing practices associated with the meditational work of Ulani. The rehuna should begin their initiation by learning these breathing methods.

The first of these techniques, the Breath of Lusteration, may be performed by the rehuna on a regular basis outside formal meditation and can, by itself, lead to deeper work, which is explored later in their training. Lusteration is the Deharan term for purification, and has its roots in the word 'lustration', which means literally 'purification by ceremony'. However, within the Deharan system, there is no connection with concepts associated with lustration, such as liberation from guilt and sin, since such notions do not exist within this system. The luster, or lustre, in this sense pertains to brightness and clarity.

The second form, the Breath of Transformation, raises energy within the body, and is required in order to summon the aurago.

The Breath of Lusteration

To begin, place the tip of your tongue to the roof of the mouth.

Then begin to breathe mindfully: push the diaphragm out when inhaling and inflate your stomach; allow it to deflate when you exhale.

This cultivates internal energy, similar to how it is enlivened during aruna, and clears out internal energy blockages. It prepares you to connect with the aurago.

When you inhale, become aware of the internal energy at your belly and visualise it as a ball or spark of life, which is fed and enlarged by your breathing.

Feel this energy flow up to the crown of your head. When you exhale, be aware of the release of this energy. Experience it flowing back down into your body, streaming around any internal blockages and gradually dissolving them, like ice being melted in water.

This procedure should feel continual and flowing. If or when you should encounter what feel like obstructions in your energy, don't attempt to remove them by force. Instead, allow the energy flow to dissolve perceived jams gradually. Assist this process by visualising the blockages being eroded and dispelled.

Once the rehuna's energy is moving freely and smoothly, they should move to the second form of breathing.

The Breath of Transformation

This reverse breathing focuses the energy required for connecting with the aurago, as well as other types of energy that the rehuna will explore later in their training. This is an empowering form of breathing.

As with the Breath of Lusteration, you should begin by touching the roof of the mouth with the tip of the tongue.

When you inhale, pull in the diaphragm and, when you exhale, expand it.

When inhaling, feel internal energy move down from your belly into your genital area and from there up the spine, to the top of the head.

When exhaling, feel the energy move down from the crown of the head back into the belly.

As you continue breathing, be aware of the energy cycling around this circuit. Allow it to move faster and faster. If you should encounter a blockage, do *not* direct the energy through it. Instead, pause and return to the Breath of Lusteration to work on breaking down the blockage.

Summoning the Aurago

If you encounter no blockages, continue to cycle the energy within the body, allowing it to intensify gradually, until you feel you cannot manage any further amplification of energy. At this point, call out mentally to the aurago and invite it to manifest. When you feel its presence, and can visualise it fully, share breath with it. This will help open psychic doors within your mind.

After the sharing of breath, ask the aurago to lead you upon a journey, where you will discover new directions for your spiritual work in this tier of study. Ask it also to reveal areas of the work upon which you need to concentrate. For each individual the spiritual direction to which they are pointed will be different.

Upon leaving the meditation, it's common to be unable to

recall every detail of what you experienced. However, irrespective of what you remember, the experience will still prime you to begin a deeper exploration of agmara energy and its relation to different spiritual systems.

During the meditation, the aurago might communicate with you, so you should keep a notebook nearby to record any observations from this experience.

Once you have returned from the journey, thank the aurago for its assistance and give an offering that you feel is appropriate for it.

Return to normal consciousness.

Ascension Majhahn

The rehuna should perform a majhahn to mark their formal ascension to the Acantha caste. They may utilise any imagery or dehara or other entities they have encountered or created during their training to this point.

The rehuna should ideally write their own ascension majhahn incorporating symbols and images that have personal meaning, but an example is given as follows, which may be expanded or adapted.

Create your etheric Nayati in your usual manner and within it perform purification procedures, such as the breathing techniques you have learned and taking a ritual bath. Adorn yourself (or not) in the way you feel is appropriate for the occasion.

Within it, create a portal into an etheric realm where your Acantha ascension will take place. This could be a temple scene or an atmospheric landscape. Using the imagery of Acantha, you could perhaps walk to your destination through a forest of thorns that part before you.

When you reach your sacred place, compose yourself there and summon the Aurago. Ask it to elevate your caste to Acantha as you are now ready to progress.

You can embellish the majhahn by invoking the Dehara Vegrandis to sanctify and confirm your ascension. You could call upon all the entities with whom you've worked to attend the ceremony. The ways to augment this majhahn are limited only by your imagination. You should use it to build up a sense of occasion and importance.

The ascension itself will involve you being attuned to the symbol Acantha. The Aurago will pass this to you, through the breath, the gaze, or the hands, or even through aruna. Visualise the symbol as light that fills your being.

After this attunement, allow time to commune with the Aurago and to meditate further on your work and what might come in the future.

When you are ready, return to your etheric Nayati and end the majhahn in your usual way.

Working Within the Ethers

The Etheric Nayati

As well as performing majhahns and magari in the mundane world, the rehuna, as part of their Ulani training, moves on to performing such workings within the ethers, specifically in the etheric Nayati they began to construct during Kaimana training.

Any majhahn or magari may be performed in this way, and the only physical world action a rehuna needs to take is the construction of the Nayati in this reality beforehand. From there, they should move into the ethers, and perform whatever majhahn, magari – or even meditation – they wish within them.

The reason for undertaking this type of working is primarily to enable the rehuna to immerse themselves fully into the mindset of their deharan self, to act in that body, to work magic in that body, to use their harish enhanced senses to affect reality and the unseen worlds. A rehuna might also choose to work etherically because they feel this lends them more power to move and affect energy in the physical realm. Whatever the reason, the rehuna should incorporate this practice alongside any physical work. It might be there are certain majhahns or magari they wish to perform that lend themselves particularly well to this form of working.

As the rehuna should by this stage be experienced at creating an etheric Nayati, and perhaps already works within it regularly, they should be able to extend their practices themselves, without too much guidance from a hienama. However, learning about the experiences and creations of other rehunas is helpful, so examples of their work are offered here to try.

Expanding the Etheric Nayati

The rehuna should already be experienced in visiting their etheric Nayati, but now they should begin to regard it not just as a place of ritual and meditation, but a magical workspace. The equipment they place within it can be anything their imagination conjures that is pertinent to their magical tasks.

Before undertaking this visualisation, the rehuna should meditate in the physical Nayati about what they think and feel would be appropriate tools to place in their etheric workplace. This will give a rough map of where they should go once within the etheric realm.

The Meditation

Within your physical Nayati, visualise its etheric version forming around you, and visualise clearly your harish form sitting within it. You will now begin to add equipment to this Nayati.

If you prefer, keep your main temple room free of such items. You can create a room or rooms specifically as workshops, perhaps on another floor of the building.

To equip this room(s), you can either visualise items appearing within it, or you could summon spiritual entities to bring them to you, or you could even go hunting for them in etheric realms. That is entirely up to you.

However you acquire the items, visualise them arranged around the room. Spend some time handling them or working with them, setting them up, consecrating them, or whatever feels appropriate. Stretch the limits of your imagination into what is placed within your etheric workplace.

This meditation can be performed regularly to expand the Nayati or to strengthen its purpose.

Etheric Realms

As part of their Acantha training, the rehuna will begin to explore etheric realms, gradually extending their travels and ultimately creating their own realms for specific purposes. To begin this work, the rehuna may first visit The Garden of Night. This can be regarded as a training realm.

The Garden of Night is visited primarily to gather the Aganymphna flower, a material that may be used in the etheric Nayati. The Aganymphna is an example of a tool that can be added to a rehuna's stock of magical materials. As the rehuna becomes more experienced with exploring etheric realms, they may discover other tools, of any type, they can then transfer to their etheric Nayati.

The rehuna will have to devise and discover their own inventory of materials, but the Aganymphna and its collection provides a firm grounding in this work. It also introduces the concept of visiting etheric realms.

Aganymphna: The Sacred Flower

Aganymphna is the mystical bloom of deharan magic, and is similar to the lotus flower, which is a prime symbol of several

33

belief systems. Like the lotus, the Aganymphna is a wide-petalled water bloom that opens out from a tight bud. When the flowers bloom, they rise from beneath the surface of the water and retreat there once their time for blooming ends.

As with the lotus, the Aganymphna represents purity and beauty, but this is a night-blooming flower so lacks any associations with sunlight possessed by the lotus. Different strains of the Aganymphna possess different properties that can be useful in majhahn and magari. The blooms may be gathered and preserved in the Nayati, but for some majhahns the rehuna might feel it appropriate to use fresh blooms. As with earthly flowers, Aganymphna needed for a particular majhahn can be collected for up to two days before and kept in water in the etheric Nayati to retain their freshness.

The Aganymphna plant grows only in certain etheric realms, where a rehuna may gather it during visualised visits. The Garden of Night is especially rich with these blooms, but they can be found in most etheric realms, although often their location is hidden or they appear sporadically. The Garden of Night is a realm of lakes and forests, but wherever Aganymphna is found, all its strains are water plants.

Below the three main strains of Aganymphna are listed, but the rehuna might discover others or even create conditions within an etheric realm to create new strains for a specific purpose.

Strains of Aganymphna

White – symbolises purity, evolution, enlightenment. The white blooms only when the Moon is in the sky. It may be harvested and preserved through the application of agmara energy. It is possible to grow white Aganymphna in a properly prepared etheric Nayati that has a water feature open to moonlight. Whites are a proper offering to most dehara and should adorn altars in the etheric Nayati. In the mundane realm, lilies of any kind may be substituted to represent these blooms. Whites may be dried and used in incense and healing tinctures. It is the most versatile and preservable of the Aganymphna strains.

Azure – symbolises magical potency, dreams, visions, inner awareness, empathy and compassion. It blooms just before dawn. When harvested, an essence of its petals may be used as a narcotic to promote visions. Azures are not normally grown within a Nayati, as those which grow in the Garden of Night are of greater potency, and it is deemed more fitting to harvest and use them when required, rather than have a supply to hand. Should be used fresh, as although dried azure does retain some potency and may be used in the creation of incense, it does not compare to freshly-gathered blooms.

Crimson – symbolises passion, arunic energy, the ability to create and destroy. Crimson blooms would be used during grissecon, as their scent alone is narcotic and aphrodisiac. They are gathered from certain caves in the Garden of Night that are filled with pools. In the darkness, they sparkle with scarlet motes of light. Performing grissecon within one of these caves is considered particularly powerful.

Crimsons may be gathered and stored for a couple of days prior to use, but thereafter lose their scent and wither. Dead or dried blooms have no magical properties whatsoever.

The rehuna may visit the Garden of Night, or any other realm, to gather these blooms and then work with them in the etheric Nayati.

The Garden of Night

Construct your physical Nayati in the usual manner and then, within it, move into the etheric Nayati. Once there, construct your portal into the Garden of Night, enter into it and from there explore.

What follows is an account by a rehuna who performed this meditation, which may be used as a template for a first visit to The Garden of Night.

I entered my tower and climbed the spiral stairs to the upmost floor. Here the ceiling is domed and made of glass. Outside the weather was dull, and autumn leaves were in the air. I closed the blinds to make my Nayati dark, but for the light of a single candle. I lit floral incense and composed myself upon cushions to meditate.

A doorway appeared to me that looked like a window onto night, streaming with water, like rain. The edges of the portal were of coloured light: pale yellow, dark green, indigo. I projected my consciousness through this portal, and once on the other side I found the realm of the Night Garden. Above was a wondrous sky alight with constellations, galaxies. Great moons hung in the firmament, some with rings about them.

Around me spread trees, grass and lakes. I was drawn to a lake on my right side, and here I could see the white Aganymphna pushing up through the water in many blooms, opening their petals. Light, liquid or plasma rose from these blooms, like rain rising as opposed to falling, drip by drip.

I went to the lake, knelt down and cut the bloom of one of the smaller plants, which I put into my leather satchel.

From here I walked into the trees and the light became dimmer. The trees were black, but veined with azure light. I was now seeking the azure Aganymphna. I crossed many streams strewn with small rocks and pebbles all covered with moss. The colours now were of deepest azure and deepest green. I came to a small pool where a series of waterfalls fell down a slope of mossy rocks. The

Aganymphna grew amid the rocks, its deep blue petals dewed with drops of water. In the dark pool at my feet, water creatures swam and coiled. I threw to them some morsels of food I had in my bag and they plunged through the surface to eat them. These creatures were like naiads, half fish, slim and sinuous.

I knelt by the pool and cut a small bloom from amid the stones, which I put into my satchel.

Now I walked on deeper into the woods. The light almost went out, but then I could see ruddy glows between the dark trees. Here was the habitat of the crimson Aganymphna. Motes of scarlet light drifted around me, and I saw wondrous insects that seemed part dragon fly, part moth. I came to the mouth of a cave set round with crimson crystals emitting light. Within, after negotiating a small tunnel, I came to an open chamber, where there was another dark pool. Water cascaded down the uneven walls here that were set with crystals of many reddish hues. And here grew the crimson flower, beautiful and radiant. I knew I couldn't gather these blooms, so instead tore off part of a petal and ate it. This tasted of cherry and almond. Warmth spread through me, and I perceived a being, perhaps a dehar demitto, emerging from the walls. He gave me no name, but shared breath with me, so that I could see a matrix of red light within both our bodies, which conjoined.

When I left this cave, I found myself emerging from the trees into a tiered landscape of pools and waterfalls. Here strange plants grew in abundance, all of which I sensed had magical properties. I saw creatures I could barely describe, incredibly beautiful; flying, scampering, swimming. There were creatures like deer only larger and with elongated legs. I wandered this landscape for a while until I came to a temple, half in ruins. It was glorious in its age and its decline. Here, I saw a portal the same as the one I'd taken to enter this realm, and knew it was time to return. The portal led back to my etheric Nayati, and once there I concluded the meditation and returned to normal consciousness.

ALOYT

Aloyt: Dehar of Dreams

The Aloytic Realm

Following one visit (or more, as they choose), to The Garden of Night, the rehuna should then revisit Aloyt, the Dehar of Dreams, first encountered during Kaimana training. Now, the rehuna should concentrate more upon Aloyt's realm, Aloytia – a realm of visions, always changing, filled with the dreams of all living beings.

Aloytia may be visited in order to gain insight into a situation, almost as a form of divination, to find directions and information concerning magical work. As before, an example of another rehuna's meditation is provided, which may be used as a template, or else the rehuna may use imagery personal to them.

Upon previous visits to this dehar, I've always visualised him walking up shallow black steps, as if upon the side of a pyramid, towards a door at the top, which is the doorway into the realm of dreams. Often, all I've seen of him are his shapely dark legs and the fact that the soles of his feet are coloured with henna or some other reddish pigment.

This time, the stairway was no longer plain and dark. It was as if it was within a sumptuous palace. There was a patterned, Persian-like carpet upon the stairs in dark reds and golds. Huge globes, perhaps of glass or paper depended from a canopy overhead, and emitted a golden glow. There were wide pillars to either side of the stairs.

At the top of the stairs, Aloyt led me into a labyrinthine palace, with hundreds of rooms. He led me to a room where there was a fountain. I'm not sure whether it was actually an enclosed room or a garden in the open air. Here he bade me lie upon the most comfortable couch I've ever lain upon. There were translucent bubbles of various colours floating around me in the air, and I was aware of hara around me, but no clear details.

Each of the bubbles was a dream or a reality. Aloyt told me I could choose one to experience, and that any one of them would be good. I chose one of a shimmering peacock blue, but whatever I found within it has faded from my memory.

As with previous work with Aloyt, the rehuna should begin the visualisation as they have done so before, but this time imagining the gate to Aloytia in detail and passing through it. There, they should explore freely and perhaps, as in the account above, even sleep or dream within the realm in order to gain deeper insights.

Sikaara

The Energy System of the Body

Throughout their magical training the rehuna works with Sikaara, the system of energy centres within the body. The term for an individual centre is sikra. The sikras are animated by agmara, the living energy of the universe.

The sikras are visualised as spheres, or aganymphna blooms, of coloured light, ranging through the spectrum from violet to red. They also relate to various aspects of the endocrine system.

In addition to the seven main sikras, there are additional and lesser sikras within the body. All are connected via energy channels known as streams. In Ulani training, the rehuna will focus upon the seven main sikras, which are positioned upon a central channel corresponding to the spine.

In Sikaara, the body is regarded as possessing more than a physical aspect, having other energetic bodies that extend beyond the flesh. These are referred to as the ethereal, the astral, the cerebral and the spiritual bodies.

Adepts of Sikaara believe that if sikras are functioning properly – regarded as 'open' - then the practitioner functions properly as a living being. The sikras can become 'blocked' by negative emotion and experiences, so that agmara does not flow through the body as freely as it should. This can give rise to dysfunction, either physically or mentally, so the rehuna no longer performs at optimum level. Restoring balance to the sikras, opening them up again through meditation and healing, so that agmara flows unimpeded, begins to repair the whole system: physically, emotionally and spiritually. Opening and enlivening the sikras also aids in self-evolution.

The Correspondences of the Sikras

Nevaath: The Base Sikra

(Ground, basis, foundation) (nev-*arth*)

This sikra is fiery red in colour and is situated at the base of the spine. Its element is earth and it is associated with the sense of smell. It also relates to the inner adrenal system that controls the 'fight or flight' response. Nevaath concerns survival fears, basic instincts, the animal self, personal stability, matters of security.

Nevaath's underlying principle is physical will, as opposed to the spiritual will embodied by the highest, seventh sikra of Nimbara. When Nevaath is functioning correctly, the rehuna is grounded, connected to the earth. They enjoy life, are stable, and feel secure – since they are secure within their being.

When Nevaath is dysfunctional, the rehuna can experience feelings of fear and uncertainty, or lack fortitude and stamina. Their way to handle difficult situations may be a tendency to flare up violently. Rage is used as a defence mechanism to shroud underlying panic and fear.

Ruuvaen: the Lower Stomach or Sacral Sikra

(Soume and ouana genital organs) (roo-*vayn*)

Ruuvaen is situated above Nevaath, below the navel and relates to the sexual organs. Its colour is a radiant orange, its element is water and it corresponds to the sense of taste. This centre is concerned with sexuality, sexual energy, desire, feelings, creativity, pleasure, self-confidence, and general well-being. This centre's fundamental principle is creative reproduction – in all senses.

When Ruuvaen is healthy, the rehuna's interpersonal relationships are relaxed and fulfilling. They will be open and welcoming in all relationships with others, platonic or otherwise. While creativity might find its outer expression via other sikras, it is born in Ruuvaen, the seat of creation, both in terms of biological reproduction and the ability to be creative in all aspects of life. An actively creative rehuna will have an open and healthy Ruuvaen.

When Ruuvaen is blocked or dysfunctional, the rehuna is likely to be cold and distant, and find it difficult to relate to others, especially in a physical or sexual sense. Emotions might be suppressed or denied. Problems in Ruuvaen often originate in youth, when sexuality first becomes active. A lack of physical bonding with parents can hamper the ability to be physically close to others – even in the sense of being able to embrace a friend or family member. It can also result in a narrow and rigid outlook, and a lack of spontaneity and freedom.

Iythra: the Solar Plexus Sikra

(Will, disposition) (*ee*-thrah)

Iythra's fundamental principle is the ability to shape reality and being. It's located below the rib cage and relates to the digestive system and the pancreas. It is the sikra of the sun, and it is thought that the body absorbs solar light through it. Therefore, it can be seen as the rehuna's personal sun, the seat of personal power. In colour it is a vibrant golden yellow, and its element is fire. It corresponds to the sense of sight and relates to will power, personal power, complex emotions, perseverance and determination. Here is born the ability to project the personality and affect reality.

The sikras can be split into sections or classes: lower, middle and higher. Along with the heart and throat, the solar plexus centre forms the middle section. The desires and impulses of the lower sikras, Nevaath and Ruuvaen, are purified and elevated by the energy of Iythra.

A rehuna having an open Iythra sikra radiates happiness and confidence, which affects others around them, who will be drawn to this light. When Iythra is fully functional, the rehuna is tolerant and understanding of others, and completely comfortable with themselves. Also, if the higher chakras are open and whole, Iythra is the first of the sikras to accommodate psychic awareness, in this case involving the sense of sight.

If Iythra is closed and dysfunctional, a natural sense of leadership is perverted into the desire to manipulate and control. A rehuna afflicted in this way will have a tendency to be restless and will need to keep themselves occupied constantly, in order to escape needling sensations of inadequacy within.

Nyasava: the Heart Sikra

(Heart, centre of chest) (nee-ah-*sah*-vah)

Nyasava is the centre of the body; three above, three below. It is located in the chest and relates to the thymus gland, which regulates the lymphatic system. Its colour is green, the colour of healing, and it relates to the element of air and the sense of touch. Nyasava's underlying principles are unconditional giving and love; an elevated love that transcends all insecurities and needs.

Nyasava relates to the ability to love unconditionally, as well as compassion, wisdom, emotional stability, patience, tolerance, and inner balance. It affords the ability to perceive beauty in the world around us. Nyasava is also the sikra of great healing.

When Nyasava is functional and open, the rehuna has the

ability to affect the world around them for the better. They will radiate natural warmth of being and sincerity, will 'feel' trustworthy to others and have the gift to instil hope. Just being near the rehuna can make others feel better within themselves.

But when Nyasava is dysfunctional, the rehuna may have a tendency to attach strings to all that they give. None of their giving is without condition, which may easily result in them being disappointed and hurt. Or the dysfunction can manifest as an inability to experience and give love freely, even to the extent of finding such things embarrassing and awkward. A closed Nyasava can make the rehuna a closed individual, apparently friendly to all, but somehow distant and cold.

Raatha: the Throat Sikra

(Throat, gullet) (*rah*-thuh)

Raatha is situated in the throat and relates to the thyroid gland and metabolism. Its colour is blue and its element is ether. It relates to the sense of hearing. The underlying principle of this sikra is communication; of ideas, thoughts and feelings.

This sikra relates to communication, sensitivity, expression of creativity, eloquence, and the ability to listen. As the last sikra between the lower and middle centres and the higher sikras of the third eye and crown, Raatha can be seen as a kind of bridge. The ideas and creative thoughts of the higher centres express themselves through Raatha.

Raatha enables the rehuna to reflect upon and analyse their thoughts and feelings. Through this, they can connect with their cerebral body and begin to discern the different layers of the etheric self. When functioning correctly, this sikra enables clear and inspired expression. Ether is an element 'higher' than earth, air fire and water.

Raatha concerns silence as much as communication. It

embodies the ability to listen to the inner voice, and in some ways enable a healthy distance from any immediate desires and needs so that they can be examined objectively.

When Raatha is dysfunctional, the link of communication between mind and body is blocked. The rehuna will be unable to reflect coherently on their thoughts and actions, and might be confused by unresolved feelings and conflicts, lacking the ability to analyse them. They might find it difficult to communicate – either by being shy and silent or else noisy and repetitive, unable to hold an audience. A fully blocked Raatha will result in utter inability to express deeply held thoughts and feelings. The words cannot be released, but are held back and suppressed within a rigid throat.

Ivlizaar: the Third Eye Sikra

(Centre of forehead) (*Iv*-lee-zaah)

Ivlizaar and Nimbara (the Crown) form the two highest centres of the energy body. Both can be said to be the seat of the 'third eye', but they may be imagined as a whole in respect of this function. Ivlizaar is situated in the middle of the forehead, above and between the eyes. It relates to the pituitary gland and extra-sensory perception. Its colour is indigo and its underlying principle is self-awareness and self-knowledge.

This is the sikra of the third eye, awareness, perception, intuition, imagination, far sight and time. Ivlizaar is the seat of the higher mental faculties and the mental ability to affect reality.

During Ulani traning, the rehuna opens and enlivens all the previous sikras in order to have a fully functioning Ivlizaar centre. This blossoming is a natural result of working upon the sikras gradually, up from Nevaath to Raatha. Once Ivlizaar begins to awake, the rehuna experiences heightened psychic awareness and intuition and acquires the ability to see through reality, to be aware of the nature of the universe.

Spirituality will feel natural and right, but at the same time they will appreciate the usefulness of logical thought and analysis. A truly functional Ivlizaar creates the mystical scientist – an individual who is curious about the workings of reality, and explores them intellectually, but who at the same time appreciates the wondrous mystery of creation, and all that is beyond normal perception.

When Ivlizaar is dysfunctional and blocked, the rehuna may become overly intellectual and devoid of any appreciation of spirituality, which will most likely be dismissed as imaginary. The rehuna may become overly vain and proud of their intellect. They might exhibit a tendency of always believing themselves to be right, regarding those who disagree with them as stupid. Such a rehuna will not be open to new ideas that challenge their ingrained beliefs, and can be aggressive in defending them. Their world view may be conventional and narrow, and the only reality that exists for them is that of the five physical senses. They will have no awareness of anything beyond that.

Nimbara: the Crown Sikra

(Crown of the head) (nim-*bah*-rah)

Nimbara is located in the centre of the skull, although the sikra is often visualised as existing just above the crown, outside the body. Its colour is generally seen as violet, although it is also pure white light, the entire spectrum. It corresponds to the pineal gland. This centre relates to the seat of consciousness, the higher self. It is the sikra of empathy and true bliss through understanding. In Nimbara all the aspects of the lower sikras are united.

When Nimbara begins to open, the rehuna starts to achieve true enlightenment. If this sikra isn't functioning fully, it's not likely to be 'blocked', but simply inactive. An open Nimbara means awareness of the true self and a connectedness with the whole of creation. The rehuna will see themselves as part of the interconnected whole.

It is difficult, if not inappropriate, to attempt to describe the consequences of an open Nimbara, simply because its opening is a personal journey for each rehuna, and their experiences of it will be different. Its opening is a lifelong process of revelation, awareness and understanding. All the work a rehuna puts into enlivening and refining the lower sikras contributes towards this ultimate blossoming, an ongoing process of discovery.

Sikaara Meditations

The rehuna should work upon the sikras throughout Ulani training and beyond. Meditations on each sikra are provided below. The rehuna may begin by concentrating upon a single sikra, beginning with Nevaath at the base of the spine, and over subsequent meditation sessions work up to Nimbara. Ultimately, the opening of the sikras, once blockages have been dispelled, can be practiced daily as one meditation.

Nevaath Meditation

Compose yourself for meditation and focus upon Nevaath. See its colour glowing vibrant red, and intend that the purpose of your meditation is to enliven and open it. Concentrate upon the positive aspects of the sikra – connectedness with the earth, a sense of belonging and security, groundedness, inner strength. See the colour of the sikra expanding outwards; vivid, strong and alive. Spin the sikra in a clockwise direction, all the time visualising it is becoming healthier and more open.

Ruuvaen Meditation

The second sikra is the seat of creativity and desire. If survival, found in the first sikra, is the fundamental drive behind the psyche, then desire and the manifestation of desires is the second. The urge to create is an innate quality, whether that is through all forms of artistic expression, including the ways rehuna organises their life, or the drive to reproduce the species. In a functioning sikra, desires are made manifest. Success through creative endeavours, in whatever occupation the rehuna has, gives the freedom to enjoy life more, whether that is through fulfilment of the self or release from material worries.

Another important aspect of working on Ruuvaen is learning to be focused. The rehuna may have creative ideas bursting like fountains from their mind, but needs to build firm foundations for these ideas and work on them in a logical order, one at a time. Scattered energy does not manifest results as well as focused energy.

When working upon the sikras, imagine that the different spheres and their symbols are like lights upon a pole, one above the other. Begin your meditations by visualising Nevaath and its light reaching up towards Ruuvaen. Activate Nevaath by filling it with the energy of agmara. See its colour grow brighter; it begins to spin in a clockwise direction, shooting off rays of brilliant red light. As this occurs it invigorates the sikra and opens it.

Now visualise Ruuvaen, and draw agmara up from Nevaath into it. See the colour grow brighter and the sikra begin to spin in a clockwise direction. It too benefits from this procedure, becoming more active and healthy.

See the two sikras as connected; the foundation of the self, with its basic survival instincts, reaching up for desire and creativity – that which separates you from animals.

Meditate for some minutes upon the qualities of Ruuvaen and how they function within you. Call upon the wisdom of the aurago to discern whether this sikra is not as open as it could be. Use this meditation to open the sikra to full functionality, gradually and as often as you are able.

51

Iythra Meditation

Iythra is the seat of the will, decision-making, the projection of the rehuna's power in reality. It is assertiveness, determination and persistence. It is the ability to finish what was started, to have the courage of convictions and to take responsibility for actions.

You began your sikra work with Nevaath and the basics of survival, reaching up for Ruuvaen and desire. Iythra is the means by which you realise these desires.

Begin your meditation by visualising Nevaath, its light reaching up towards Ruuvaen. Activate Nevaath by filling it with agmara. See its colour grow brighter; it begins to spin in a clockwise direction, shooting off rays of brilliant red light.

Now visualise Ruuvaen, and draw agmara up from Nevaath to vitalise it. See the colour grow brighter and the sikra begin to spin in a clockwise direction.

Draw agmara up into Iythra. See the sikra begin to spin and grow stronger. The energy invigorates and opens the sikra.

As with the previous sikras, meditate upon Iythra and discern its level of functionality, calling upon the aurago for guidance if it feels appropriate.

Nyasava Meditation

The rehuna may have experiences with others that have scarred them, and find it difficult to forgive and let go of the negative feelings surrounding the situation. Similarly, they might harbour feelings of regret and guilt over past actions and find it hard to forgive themselves. Working on Nyasava helps with these issues.

When working with Nyasava, the rehuna should concentrate on their connectedness with all other living beings, through the medium of agmara.

Nyasava can be seen as the first of the 'higher' sikras.

After concerns of the inner self, the energy now reaches outwards to embrace the universe. Projected will without compassion and empathy can be tyrannical; Iythra needs the subtle emanations of Nyasava to remain stable and just.

Begin by enlivening the other sikras, starting with Nevaath. The energy vitalises the red sikra of survival, rising through the orange of desire and creativity, through the golden yellow of projected will into the green heart centre. Visualise the 'flame' of your heart sikra and work upon strengthening it, imagining that it grows brighter within you. It is important to love yourself as much as extending compassion to others. Spend some time nurturing yourself, by feeding Nyasava with agmara.

As with the previous sikras, meditate upon Nyasava and discern its level of functionality, calling upon the aurago for guidance if it feels appropriate.

Raatha Meditation

As Nyasava tempers the energy of Iythra and projected will, so the light of truth and honest communication enhances and purifies the rehuna's experiences. Raatha helps the rehuna discern what is truth and what is delusion, what is wishful thinking and what actually 'is'. The rehuna may believe they have the power to change their reality, but first they must be able to view that reality objectively, not coloured too strongly by what they want to believe or what they fear might be so.

The rehuna might regularly bite back words and seethe quietly over situations, because they fear the consequences of speaking honestly. Repressed energy can build in Raatha, eventually blocking the sikra.

When working on Raatha, begin by enlivening the other sikras, starting with Nevaath. The energy vitalises the red sikra of survival, rising through the orange of desire and creativity, through the golden yellow of projected will into the green heart centre of Nyasava. The energy then rises into the throat and Raatha, the seat of truth and communication. Visualise the brilliant blue of this sikra. Feed it with agmara and see it begin to spin. As you meditate upon the issues that concern you, chant softly 'this is really so'. Ask for truth to be shown to you. But remember there are many truths; what is true for you might not be true for another.

As with the previous sikras, meditate upon Raatha and discern its level of functionality, calling upon the aurago for guidance if it feels appropriate.

Ivlizaar Meditation

Working upon Ivlizaar awakens the rehuna's latent psychic abilities, and sharpens the senses. It also nourishes creativity.

One of the most important functions of a healthy Ivlizaar is having discernment about what is real and what is not. If the rehuna exists wholly in the realm of dreams they may become lost in them. They need to be able to discriminate between illusion and reality, and work upon Ivlizaar to achieve this objective and clear sight of the self.

Another aspect of working with this sikra is attunement to the significance of signs and symbols around the rehuna in everyday life. If the rehuna is awake and alive in the world, paying attention to the details around them, so these signs will become more apparent and visible.

The rehuna has worked through all the lower sikras and now enter the realms of the cosmos, the higher spheres. Ivlizaar is the penultimate centre before the seventh; it is the gateway to the stars.

Begin by enlivening the other sikras, starting with Nevaath. The energy vitalises the red sikra of survival, rising through the orange of desire and creativity, through the golden yellow of projected will into the green heart centre of Nyasava. The energy then rises into the throat and Raatha; the seat of truth and communication. From here, it rises into Ivlizaar. Truth is enhanced by insight. Visualise the deep indigo light of this sikra. Feed it with agmara and see it begin to spin. Open yourself to what ideas and images come to you.

As with the previous sikras, meditate upon Ivlizaar and discern its level of functionality, calling upon the aurago for guidance if it feels appropriate.

Nimbara Meditation

Begin by enlivening the other sikras, starting with Nevaath. The energy vitalises the red sikra of survival, rising through the orange of desire and creativity, through the golden yellow of projected will into the green heart centre of Nyasava. The energy then rises into the blue throat centre, Raatha, the seat of truth and communication. From here, it ascends into the indigo light of Ivlizaar, and the inner sight of intuition, thereafter rising to above the head to Nimbara. Visualise the vivid violet light of this sikra. Feed it with agmara and see all of the sikras begin to spin.

Concentrate upon the energy rising upwards through all the sikras and experience what each sikra represents as you do so. In Nimbara lies the completed whole and the bridge to further experience and knowledge.

When meditating in Nimbara – and while focussing on this sikra you are *in* it – focus without strain upon surrendering desires and attachments to physical things and other beings. Simply *be* yourself, unfettered, full of potential and creativity. In this place, there are no demands put upon you. It is the realm of pure, liberated personal experience.

Once you have existed in this state for some minutes, noting all that you feel and perceive, gradually move your focus to connection with all that exists, your part within the universal whole.

When you feel ready, visualise the energy of Nimbara beginning to cascade back down through the other sikras, bringing with it spiritual nourishment. Ground the energy in Nevaath.

Now visualise that the whole energy system is a constant cycle of movement, as energy travels up from Nevaath to Nimbara and back down again. Thus the grounding of Nevaath anchors the experience of Nimbara, and Nimbara inspires the mundane qualities of Nevaath. Each of the sikras is of equal importance, supporting each other. Focus upon each in turn and contemplate how they enliven and enrich each other.

Dehara Demitto of Acantha

Dehara of both major and minor character are continually invented for spiritual purposes, and this extends to the utilisation and adaptation of personalities from Wraeththu lore, who possess strong characteristics and traits. Any Wraeththu figures can be used for this purpose.

Abrimel

Abrimel represents the guilty and the innocent. If a rehuna is guilty of wrong-doing, Abrimel requires them to take action in restitution for what they have done. He is all-seeing and cannot be deceived. He is called upon when seeking justice, but also as a guide for the rehuna focusing on internal work, who might need to deal with unresolved issues. Abrimel will bring such issues to the fore, enabling the rehuna to face them with courage and to see the reality behind them. Abrimel facilitates the rehuna to experience what they *need* to feel, such as the emotion of shame: to feel it in a raw and pure state, in order to work through it.

As the ascension to the next stage of Ulani, Pyralis, Abrimel will also lead the rehuna to his chesnari, Ponclast, to embark upon an underworld journey.

Characteristics of Abrimel

In Wraeththu lore, Abrimel is the exiled son of Tigron Pellaz and Tigrina Caeru of the Aralisian dynasty. He represents guilt and innocence. He was an innocent – a harling caught up in the conflict of parents, which scarred him. He was spurned by his father, and considered his hostling weak and incapable of standing up for him. His disillusionment with his tribe, the Gelaming, propelled him to ally with Ponclast, erstwhile leader of the warlike Varrs. He sought to destroy his own dynasty, and after failing in this endeavour was captured and imprisoned. Yet in later years, he was redeemed.

As a dehar, he sees directly into the heart of a rehuna, beyond self-delusion, ignorance and misinformation. He demands the rehuna takes responsibility for their actions and reactions and that – should it be appropriate – restorative action be taken. In a magical sense, he may be invoked when seeking justice, but his main purpose for the rehuna working on Ulani ascension is as a guide. He aids the rehuna in facing issues they might wish to avoid, or that they feel incapable of resolving. He allows the rehuna to see, impartially, the reality of situations in their lives. If a rehuna should be experiencing the emotion of shame, Abrimel assists in seeing through that emotion, to the issues that lie behind it. Often, they are groundless, and shame is merely a result of conditioning in early life that must be confronted and worked through. Other times, a rehuna might well have acted selfishly or cruelly, and restitution might have to be made, if only through self-purification and acceptance.

Abrimel is also a dehar who may be approached to assist with the scars and traumas left by abuse, both physical and mental. In Wraeththu lore, he is often a bitter creature, but can assist with this emotion by helping the rehuna to see through bitterness to its cause, and thus neutralise it.

In appearance, he is tall, lean and dark-haired, somewhat ascetic of feature. His long hair is drawn back from his face. His ambience is severe; he has no nurturing aspect. He dresses formally, in clothes that will appear rather stiff.

Xynlis the Gatekeeper

Xynlis is a dehar of transition, portals, gateways, journeys of passage, and of beginnings and endings. He is also associated with time, as in the sense of passing from the present to the future, or from the past to the future, or transition through time from one state of being to another. Within Ulani training, he is invoked to open gateways into the deeper realms and represents entry into higher levels of learning.

The gatekeeper can take many forms, and there is no set description of his appearance. He may appear differently to the rehuna on separate occasions but often, as with other deities of his nature, he may possess two or more faces, as he can see into the future and the past, as well as into other realms of reality.

The Cloister of Abrimel Meditation

This working forms the conclusion of the Acantha stage of Ulani. Before the rehuna may embark upon Pyralis, by undertaking the underworld journey to Xephelax, they must first purify themselves and identify their flaws. This is not a procedure to eliminate weaknesses, but simply to become aware of them, thus removing their power to sabotage the rehuna's life-plans and relationships. An inability to be accountable for one's actions is a weakness, as is a lack of self-responsibility; if left unattended, entities of the underworld may fix upon them, destabilising the ascension to Pyralis. Therefore, preparation for Xephelax involves a searing degree of self-honesty. If ignoble traits or actions are denied or ignored, they become exploitable weaknesses. Strength cannot take root in polluted ground. It is not a fault to have weaknesses, for no rehuna is a perfect being, but it is a failing to deny or hide from them. Acceptance gives power.

Abrimel's function is to assist the rehuna in uprooting and identifying negative traits and mechanisms that have become entrenched in the psyche, sometimes very deeply.

In Wraeththu lore, the Cloister of Abrimel is the area in which he was confined after the second fall of Fulminir. High-ranking hara who commit serious crimes are generally exiled to etheric realms that are not prisons in the literal sense. Wrongdoers are removed from the earthly realm, and here encouraged to become aware of their actions and identify what impulses and conditioning instigated them. This forms part of their rehabilitation.

The Meditation

Compose yourself for meditation in the usual manner and pass into your etheric Nayati.

Call upon Xynlis the Gatekeeper to open a portal for you into the Cloister of Abrimel. Say:

'Astale, Xynlis of Many Faces, I call you here to grant me passage to the Cloister of Abrimel. You, who have command over doorways, and the power to open and close all portals, and the power of movement and transition, conjure for me the gateway to the Cloister of Abrimel, in the name of the Aghama, the star and your sovereign. '

Visualise Xynlis manifesting before you and then opening up the gateway, which appears as a shimmering portal before you. Pass through the portal, and give Xynlis a token as you do so. This may be visualised as a coin, or some other appropriate currency.

The Cloister is an ancient temple complex that appears to be constructed of different architectural styles, some familiar to you, some alien. A proportion of the buildings are ruins, while others appear newly-constructed.

Above you is a dark and starry sky, with three moons, one white, one pale blue, one tinged with red. These represent wisdom, compassion and courage.

The area seems deserted. You can hear no animals or night-birds and perceive no sign of any other living thing. A great stillness hangs over the scene.

You are drawn to a particular area of the complex, which comprises arches, columns and shadowed areas – Abrimel's domain within this realm. The precise architecture and style of the structures are personal to you – allow them to manifest in your visualisation freely.

A figure walks slowly towards you from the shadows, tall and severe in appearance. Abrimel comes to you in the form of The Accuser. He stands silently before you and you say,

'Astale, Abrimel, I stand before you to face my truths. I give you leave to accuse, to voice all that is hidden or silenced. Speak to me the deepest knowledge of my heart.'

At this stage, allow yourself to be open to whatever this dehar might say to you. Some of his words will inevitably sting, but remain focused. Do not wince away or allow emotions to take control. Listen impartially and without judgement.

Abrimel will name negative traits and/or actions and will hand to you an object representing each one, which you arrange before you so you can examine them from a detached perspective.

He will say 'Do you own this ***?' (whatever trait or action) And you reply, 'Yes, it is mine. I accept it from you.'

Each of the objects Abrimel names and gives to you are a part of your being, experiences that have shaped you.

Abrimel says:

'Without darkness, light has no meaning.
Without pain, pleasure has no context.
To work good, you must know evil's face.
To heal, you must know the nature of smiting.
The true adept owns all their experiences with gratitude.'

Contemplate how everything you do in life contributes towards learning. When you look back at times when you acted badly, cruelly, stupidly or ignorantly, it's important not to be overwhelmed by shame and guilt but to learn from these situations, to be aware of why you behaved or thought or felt in that way, and how you can avoid repeating them. What triggered them? Be honest.

Meditate on the crippling nature of guilt and shame; blockages that prevent growth. Handle each object Abrimel gives to you that represents a past negative action, thought or feeling. Say, 'this situation did not make me grow, but now I see it as it was, and accept its consequences. Now I release it.'

Then visualise the object dissolving into mist, passing into you, part of you, but harmless.

This process is not about making restitution or seeking forgiveness from others. Those are actions for the mundane world. This meditation simply involves taking responsibility for your own actions without judgement. It concerns understanding the behavioural mechanisms within you that make you react out of habit or conditioning. It is about breaking this conditioning and acting with true independence and insight. These are the gifts of Abrimel the Accuser.

After you have completed this part of the meditation, spend some time within Abrimel's realm and speak with him further if you wish to.

When you are ready, return to normal consciousness and close your etheric nayati.

The aim of this majhahn is that you do not undertake the ascension to Pyralis in a state where surprises might be sprung upon you, incidents surfacing that you hadn't confronted during your visit to the Cloister of Abrimel. If you feel it's appropriate to repeat this majhahn then do so. There might well be layers of experiences to penetrate.

Pyralis

The Path of the Pyralisit

Pyralis is the Way of Fire. It demands that the rehuna go deeply into their own psyche, wrestle with inner demons, and purify themselves of negative traits. The fire of Pyralis is used to burn away dross. It is the fire of the Phoenix, and from its ashes the rehuna arises renewed.

Fire can take many forms: the crackle of electricity, the raging red flames of burning wood, the cold blue fire of the ethers. Within the etheric realms, the rehuna may experience different kinds of fire. The dehar Agave can be called upon as guide and protector in certain situations, or dehara demitto may reveal themselves to the rehuna upon their journeys.

A rehuna may not become a hienama if they are slaves to the lower emotions, such as pride, envy, jealousy, insecurity and lust (the latter in its sense of meaningless acquisitiveness or self-gratification). They cannot attain the higher tiers of the system if they seek to have power over others, because that is a weakness. The truly powerful do not have to exert dominance in order to feel safe and in control of their reality. They exist within the haven of honest self-awareness, and in that state the desire to control others – or to feel 'better' or stronger than others – is meaningless.

To a certain degree Pyralis must also burn away the tendency to attachment; not to render the rehuna a cold and emotionless being, but to put their emotions in context, to live them fully and without the debilitating insecurities that can sully pure emotions.

The Symbol Pyralis

The second symbol of Ulani represents the refining nature of spiritual fire. While the fire of Pyralis may burn the rehuna, and in different ways, it also has healing properties. If the journey through the thorns of Acantha should leave what might feel similar to 'open sores' in the psyche, Pyralis cauterises those wounds and mends them, thus speeding recovery from the sometimes arduous work previously undertaken.

In the rehuna's visualisations, and visits to etheric realms, they may bathe in sacred waters to find solace and be soothed, but to bathe in the sacred fires of Pyralis can be equally refreshing.

The function of the Pyralis symbol is to evoke the fire of this tier with its strengthening and healing properties. Holding the fire within themselves, the rehuna may venture fearlessly into Xephelax, the underworld, which is the core of Ulani training.

In majhahn, Pyralis can be used to instil greater strength into a magical working, especially when the properties of strong healing and cleansing are required. It focuses the white light of agmara into a channel of purifying flame.

Pyralis is drawn by beginning at the foot and working up and through the symbol. The two short vertical lines are added last. The symbol may be visualised as three dimensional, with the tail being closest to the eye. The vertical lines can be visualised as one on each side of the line they cross.

Meditation upon Pyralis

The rehuna should meditate upon the symbol of Pyralis for at least a week before embarking upon the underworld journey. While they may devise their own meditation for this purpose, an example is given as follows for interacting with the symbol.

Fire Walk

In a darkened room, gaze into a candle flame for some minutes, emptying your mind of all mundane thoughts. Focus upon the purity of the flame.

Close your eyes, and concentrate on the image of the flame, enlarging it before you, until it becomes an oval portal of fire. Draw the Pyralis symbol over it, and see this as drawn in flame. Rise up and walk through the portal. The fire does not

Storm Constantine & Taylor Ellwood

burn you, but rather you take on aspects of the fire as a garment. You walk beyond the portal robed in flame.

Beyond the portal, you find the path of Pyralis. Visualise this as you will, and walk upon it. Interact with any entities you might find there.

When you are ready, return to normal consciousness and conclude the meditation.

Revisiting the Dehara

At the start of Pyralis, the rehuna should revisit the Dehara Vegrandis in order to prepare themselves for majhahns later in the caste training. What follows is an example from a rehuna's personal experience:

I created the Nayati in the usual manner and drew the symbol of Pyralis to symbolise my further journey into Ulani, asking the dehara for aid in this.

I visualised going to a square, high temple, of four quarters, each of which was relevant to the dehara.
  I saw the temple as standing in wide flat gardens, surrounded by canals, fountains and trees.
  I entered through the south portal and, after passing through a small ante-chamber, found myself in a large room, dominated by a statue of Agave, who had raised arms and wielded a curved sword. Paths led round either side of the

71

statue and behind it. Here I found a large dark chamber, lit only by flickering bowls of fire. At its end Agave stood upon a bed of coals. On either side of the room I saw statues of stylised seated red panthers. I also picked up an impression of the serpent being a creature of Agave. The ceiling of this room was lost in shadow but bowls of fire on decorative chains hung from it.

I approached the dehar across the living coals and he imparted to me that his function in my training was to help purge insecurities and fears, to transcend petty human concerns, to live in the moment. He was 'The Now' of the four dehara. His fire should be called upon to augment will, tenacity and courage.

Behind Agave was a sphere of swirling black light, highlit with gleams of turquoise, red and white. I pushed my face into this, and it was like stretching a membrane, then I could walk through it into another deharan realm.

This was the temple of Miyacala, only one room this time, high-ceilinged and white. I had the impression of glittering gems everywhere, cups spilling with the most scintillating diamonds, columns of glistering light. At the end of this room stood Miyacala, and in addition to his blind eyes, he had an open third eye in the middle of his forehead. When I approached him, he told me that my future self would assist me during my work. I took this to mean space/time magic, and also perhaps that the self I was now could heal the selves damaged in the dark years between my previous work and now.

Miyacala is 'The Future' of the four major dehara. I caught a glimpse of a being of blue light, which I imagined was one of my selves. This could also be a self beyond life when true wisdom is attained. Or a far future self beyond corporeal form.

Behind Miyacala, I saw an oval of shimmering air, quite dark in appearance, and only slightly less tall than myself. I passed through this and found myself in the realm of Aruhani. This took the form of an immense, deep cavern that was roofless, but the opening was so far above that light in the chamber was very dim. Water ran down the walls, which were of beautiful stone, mottled black and brown with seams of mica, and smudged with iridescent lichen and moss. Vines also hung down the walls, dripping with water. The water fell in from above, over the lip of the cavern. In the centre of the chamber was a pool and here sat Aruhani, the water falling around him. He appeared as I usually see him, with black skin and a mass of long braids. This was an earthy realm but water was also prevalent. Aruhani said to me that he represented 'The Past' in my work, and that this was a mix of beneficial and non-beneficial influences. The past is generally seen as bad as we dwell on mistakes, stupidity, gullibility, and other faults we perceive sullied our lives. We focus on those who betrayed and lied to us, those who were disloyal, and catastrophic bad luck in all aspects of our lives. We tend to forget the good experiences, the kind people, the lovers who helped us evolve, the friends who were loyal, and the times when luck went in our favour. Aruhani's influence is to balance the past, to let it go in some respects, but also to appreciate its gifts and how they helped make me the wiser person I am now.

A swarm of butterflies spiralled down from the open air and fluttered around Aruhani, making patterns that were symbols and sigils. I couldn't memorise any of these before they vanished, though, or morphed into something new.

Behind Aruhani, I perceived a hidden exit that led into a short tunnel. This took me to the lip of a sloping cliff, or mountainside, with a series of waterfalls and rapids. I took on a semi aquatic form and dived into this, tumbled down the stream like an otter. It was pleasurable and refreshing, the scenery around me breathtakingly beautiful. Eventually I was tossed over a cliff edge and plummeted down an immense, roaring waterfall, diving into an ocean at its foot. This was a cerulean sea, and the realm of Lunil. I saw a water temple floating on the surface, with intricate columns and other decorations, somewhat delicate in appearance. Lunil appeared to me as a dehar of dark turquoise colouring. He told me to look beneath the surface of the ocean, and when I did so, I saw multiple objects, images, even words. Lights flickered on and off, or were creatures that swam by me, mere ideas or thoughts. The sea was absolutely crowded with glowing data, if it could be called that. Lunil said it is the Sea of Possibilities, known to artists and poets and philosophers. In it all ideas spring forth into creation. Or ideas are born there. Of the dehara, Lunil is 'Possibility', limitless potential, which should work with the qualities of the other dehara.

I experienced many thoughts and ideas in this realm, which unfortunately did not linger once I left it. I returned to the original temple and exited into the gardens. Here I met my aurago. We walked together and conversed more. Shortly after this, I concluded the meditation and returned to normal consciousness.

Purging by Fire

Majhahns to Deal with Conflict, Pain & Justice

The rehuna in training often feels that negative feelings, such as anger, resentment and jealousy should be removed from their being, as they are unevolved and the emotions of ignorance. However, it can't be denied that conflicts arise in life, and the rehuna might occasionally be faced with situations where discord has to be settled, even when resolution seems impossible. The actions, thoughts and feelings of others can be destructive, and sometimes no amount of tolerance or good will can ameliorate the situation or make the damage disappear. In some cases, the rehuna must act decisively to rid their lives, or the lives of others who ask for assistance, of negative or harmful influences.

The rehuna does not have to resort to curses or hexes, but they are entitled to protect themselves or others when a situation merits it.

The Majhahn of Forgiveness and Banishment

An aspect of Pyralis, the way of fire, is to purge by flame harmful and lingering aspects of the past. When rifts occur, there is often hostile action on both sides. This particular majhahn is for those situations when angry feelings have escalated and vehement, perhaps rash, words have been exchanged between two or more individuals. Damage has been done. The rehuna might have felt justifiably driven to retaliate, to seek allies by disparaging their opponent. They might, with hindsight, realise that their own actions and feelings contributed to the hostility just as much as the actions of others. This majhahn is undertaken to heal and release historical hurts. The instructions can be adapted to suit whatever situation a rehuna wishes to heal.

The act of forgiveness is often difficult, for a rehuna might mistakenly believe it implies they condone what happened to them, thus leaving them open to being abused in the same manner again. And for the same reason they might hold onto anger and unhappiness because they don't want to forget what happened. Yet this allows the past to continually affect them. They also poison themselves subtly, by harbouring negative feelings within. The rehuna should ask themselves: when they can't forgive another, who has the power in that situation? Forgiving an adversary doesn't mean the rehuna has to 'turn the other cheek' or condone manipulative or aggressive behaviour.

Performing a forgiveness majhahn allows the rehuna to set aside lingering regret or bitterness. The rehuna will no longer pour energy into the antagonist or the historical situation. They make a conscious choice to discard feelings of resentment and move on. A final benefit of this majhahn is that the rehuna also forgives themselves. Sometimes, a rehuna might feel angry for getting involved a situation, for not being alert and aware enough to protect themselves, or for their own actions that caused hurt to another. The act of self-forgiveness releases these emotions and repairs self-esteem.

*"I woke up in a bad mood. I'd been dreaming about someone, who long ago had done bad things to me. I usually don't think about them, but occasionally I remember what they did and feel a lot of anger toward them. Each time I feel that anger, I also feel frustration, because there doesn't seem to be much I can do to vent that anger toward them. Today was no different, until I meditated in my Nayati and realised that my real source of frustration wasn't what that person had done, but my choice to brood on their actions. I felt like I had no control, but if anything I was giving **them** control – as well as a lot of my own energy – by continuing to dwell on the past, instead of focusing on the present and future.*

"To rectify this problem, I knew it was time to stop investing energy into the past and start focusing on what I could do about it now. I decided to enact the majhahn of forgiveness, which would also serve to release and banish the energy I was preserving in those historical situations. I couldn't talk with the person I was forgiving as they are no longer in in my life. But by forgiving them, as well as myself for my part in the situation, I could release the connection between us, and then banish them from my mind. It wasn't just that I didn't want to feel anger, but that I didn't want this emotion to continue controlling me, especially concerning situations that had occurred long ago.

"That evening, I went again to my Nayati and called into it the Aghama, Aruhani, Miyacala, Lunil, and Agave: Aghama as Dehar of Space and Spirit; Aruhani as Dehar of Death, Rebirth and Aruna; Miyacala as Dehar of Initiation and Magic; Lunil as Dehar of Flexibility and Flow; and Agave as Dehar of Protection and Healing. By asking them to create a sacred space where I could perform my majhahn of forgiveness, I felt that I was protected from any malice that those I evoked might bear me."

Preparation

Devise a personal symbol to represent the cutting of ties.

Place within your Nayati a bell, or some other instrument that might be struck and leave a lingering tone.

Have with you a crystal pendant on a thong or chain, or some other similar item of jewellery to serve the same purpose.

Write a 'litany of hurts' that lists the harms you feel were done to you.

The Majhahn

Create your Nayati in the usual manner. Sit down within it, and set the bell and crystal pendant before you. Strike the bell and call the full name of the individual you wish to forgive, to evoke their presence into your Nayati.

As the tone of the bell fades, meditate upon the antagonist and the harms they did to you – as you perceive these hurts – and also the harms you might have done to them, (as they might perceive this). Recount in absolute detail how you feel the antagonist damaged you. Then think about how you might have hurt this person in return, so that you may forgive yourself for your own actions too.

(It's not necessary or advisable to ask for forgiveness from the antagonist for your part in the events, as your perception of the past is subjective and does not necessarily reflect how the antagonist authentically felt about you or the situation.)

Chant or recite the litany of hurts, of what occurred, several times, and at the conclusion of each recital, say:

"*name*, I forgive you for your actions and I banish this connection between us. I release your energy back to you and re-claim my energy for myself. Go in peace on your journey."

Then take up the crystal pendant and wrap it around your hand, so that you may hold the crystal between your thumb and forefinger. Raise it in the air and gaze upon it. Imagine the cleansing fire of Pyralis within it. See the symbol of Pyralis within the stone.

Then, in the air before you, use the crystal to trace the

'cutting of ties' symbol you created for the majhahn. Intend that this severs any remaining connection between you and the other person. Imagine two clasped hands slowly uncurling and releasing, with each participant's energy going back to themselves.

As you banish the energy of your antagonist – who you should visualise as no longer that, but simply another person, someone you no longer have in your life – feel a weight lifting from you. Feel yourself being rejuvenated by reclaiming your own energy.

Now, say aloud: "I forgive myself for my part in this history. It is done with. It has gone from me."

Again, feel your being become lighter as any remaining negativity drains from you. Imagine it drifting from you like smoke, burned away to nothing.

The majhahn may be concluded by performing a cleansing exercise of your choice to recycle negative emotional energy into positive energy. Because you have recalled your energy from the past, you should make sure to perform a purification to cleanse any leftover negative emotions.

Variations on the Majhahn of Forgiveness

This majhahn may be enacted in several ways. The example within this grimoire involves evocation of the antagonist as a means to release the negative energy associated with past conflict, but a rehuna could choose instead to invoke the *memories* of the situation and others involved, then visualise going into these memories to forgive the antagonist and themselves.

A rehuna could also use a visualised path-working to revisit what occurred and change the outcome, in order to put it behind them and release negativity from it.

Another method could involve the burning of a candle that has been carved with symbols to represent the situation or people with which the rehuna is displeased. In this case, the rehuna should imagine all the negative emotions going into the symbols as they're being carved. Then they should light the candle, and use the fire of Pyralis as a flame of forgiveness to banish lingering and unhealthy energy.

There are many other ways this forgiveness majhahn could be performed. The rehuna may experiment with other methods to create a majhahn entirely personal to them.

The Mahallatu: Dark Riders of Justice

The Mahallatu were the Twelve, and echoed entities in earlier belief systems, as many of the dehara did. They were the archetypal dark riders, who travelled the storm winds and restless clouds to mete out justice and retribution. Their leader was Merim and his eyes were red, his hair the colour of dried blood, almost black but with a hint of meat in its depths. The Mahallatu met in the back room of an inn in a far corner of the etheric realms. In this place, a petitioner could approach them and ask for help.

I called upon the Mahallatu in my mind. The night was clear, yet I imagined strange, purple clouds, veined with harsh yellow light, drawing in from every quarter. Within the clouds, the malediction of merciless hooves, striking sparks from the air. My heartbeat increased. I could feel them drawing closer, their savage joy. I gave birth to them in the darkness, in that serene glade, beneath an imagined storm.

From 'Student of Kyme', Storm Constantine, 2008

The Mahallatu are dehara demitto of Pyralis – twelve riders of truth, retribution and justice. Their way is harsh yet just. They will not tolerate deceit or cruelty. They guard the grail of dehara, their brother Phynayel. This dehar is a deity of reconciliation, healing, unconditional love, compassion and redemption.

A rehuna should only resort to this majhahn when a situation is serious enough to merit its use. It should be employed when others have worked actively to cause damage for their own gain, or have acted malevolently through jealousy and envy, or through fear. There should be incontrovertible evidence of malicious intent and/or injury and vindictiveness. It should especially be used when the rehuna, or someone who seeks their aid, feels threatened and in danger.

Prior to this majhahn, the rehuna should meditate and seek the advice of their aurago as to whether the majhahn should proceed. There should be no doubt in the rehuna's mind, and no margin for misapprehension, delusion or selfish motives. If the rehuna should feel any uncertainty, they may also visit the Cloisters of Abrimel and ask for the truth of the situation to be made clear. If, after these precautions, the rehuna feels comfortable to proceed, they should consider it safe to do so. They should be prepared to take full responsibility for their actions, and make adequate provision that no harm befall any party involved. The purpose is to protect and dispel, not to retaliate.

This majhahn should be performed on the first night of the waning moon. The wording may be adapted if performed by a group of rehunas, or if others are present who have asked for assistance in matters of conflict and justice. It may also be reworded to reflect accurately the situation that needs to be resolved. As such, some of what follows is simply an example.

Preparation

While using a magical sword as a conduit for this majhahn is preferable, should you not have such an artefact, you may use your vakei or another magical implement that seems appropriate.

The Majhahn

Prepare your Nayati in your usual manner. When it is ready, stand in the centre and call upon the power of agmara.

MERIM OF THE MAHALLATU

In the air before you, draw the symbols of Ara, Neoma, Brynie, Acantha and Pyralis. Say:

'Ara, be the gateway
Neoma, be the shield of protection
Brynie, be the axis of grounding
Acantha, be the portal of the cosmos
Pyralis, be the flame that repels all hostile forces.'

Compose yourself in the centre of your Nayati and clear your mind. Then say:

'On this night, the moon passes from full to waning. I come to this sacred place to empower myself, to clear all obstacles from my path, to banish negative influences and stem the hostile actions and thoughts of those who stand against and oppose me. I do this in good faith and in the sight of Cosmic Law. I have called upon the dehara and now summon their night-riding allies, the Mahallatu, those warriors who have influence over matters of justice and truth, who will ride forth to right injustice. Let those who stand in their path do so at their peril.'

Stand in the middle of the circle, raise the sword before you and say firmly:

'I call upon Merim, leader of the night-riding Mahallatu,
Come forth with your kin from your realm between the realms
In the name of Aruhani, Miyacala, Agave, Lunil,
And Aghama, the Brightest Star of the Cosmos,
Surround me! Come to my aid,
Give me the power of your swords! Give me your strength!'

Raise the sword higher towards the sky and say with conviction:

'Honoured Mahallatu, Riders of the Ethers, come to me now.
I entreat you to silence slanderous tongues that speak against

me unjustly.

I entreat you to nullify the power of those who seek to cause me harm.

Come to me, mighty Mahallatu, hear my call!

Now visualise the black-cloaked Mahallatu riding upon great black sedim towards you through the sky. They each carry a drawn sword that shivers with the fire of Pyralis. They are grim and stern, and can see through all. Face them without fear. They are here to help you.

The Mahallatu form a circle around you. Feel their keen attention. They listen.

Say: 'May the fire of truth fall upon my enemies. Let their treachery be exposed. Let them face the raw reflection of themselves. And, if in the light of that reflection, they recognise their wrong-doing, bring them to the light of your hidden brother Phynayel, for there is none that might not be redeemed.'

The Mahallatu point their swords towards the sky. Their power and support is yours.

Now face each of the directions in turn, commanding with a raised sword.

'Hear my words, enemies in the East
Your influence no longer affects my life.'
I grow stronger, while your might and malice fades.'

'Hear my words, enemies in the South
Your spiteful words no longer affect my life.'
I grow stronger, while your might and malice fades.'

'Hear my words, enemies in the West
By the power of the Mahallatu, I return to you the ill will you send against me.'
I grow stronger, while your might and malice fades.'

'Hear my words, enemies in the North
Know that I am empowered and shielded by the dehara and
the mighty Mahallatu
I grow stronger, while your might and malice fades.'

Lay down the sword before you. Now chant again, beginning
in a slow whisper, building in strength, speed and volume:

Visualise as you do so these mighty forces riding out to do as
you desire.

'Ma ha la tu. Ma ha la tu. Ma ha la tu.'

When you feel energy circling around you has reached its
peak, throw up your arms and release the power to do its
work, with a wordless cry.

Now stand silently and visualise yourself filling up with the
cleansing fire of Pyralis that pushes out into the room and
beyond. It fills you with power and strength. See yourself as
immensely tall, vibrant, brimming with energy and power.
Nothing can stand in your path and no one can harm you.

Sit within your Nayati and toast the dehara.

Conclude the majhahn in your usual manner.

Agave Majhahn of Justice

This majhahn is milder in nature than that seeking the aid of the Mahallatu. It should be performed when a rehuna has been wronged, or finds themselves dwelling on the damaging actions someone committed against them. This majhahn is not for revenge, but instead to bring justice to the other person, without harming them.

For this majhahn, the rehuna evokes Agave, Dehar of Fire and Protection. Agave's purpose in this instance is to help the rehuna to balance the karmic scales with the other person involved, while also purifying them of any lingering emotions that would otherwise be poisonous to their systems. As with all majhahns in this grimoire, the wording may be changed to accurately represent a rehuna's situation.

Preparation

Required equipment:

Squares of papyrus, parchment or paper – one for each individual this majhahn is directed towards.
A pen or pencil.
A censer.
Matches or a lighter.

On each parchment square draw a sigil or symbol that represents the individual who caused harm. The sigil should be the letters of the person's full name, (or an abbreviation of their name, such as initials), fashioned into a symbol. You should also devise a pronunciation of the symbol, which isn't quite the name of the person, but is similar yet with a slight discordance.

The Majhahn

Once the sigils have been prepared, construct your Nayati in the usual manner.

Sit within the centre of your Nayati and call upon Agave. Visualise him coming forth from the south to be with you. Say aloud:

'Astale Agave, Dehar of Fire and Protection.
I call on you to balance the scales of justice.
I call on you to release within me any emotional connection to (name of person).
Purge from me unhappiness, anger and hatred,
Reflect it back to the one who caused it,
so they may learn whatever lessons are needed
to help them become a better person.
I release (name of sigil) to (name of person),
and ask you to burn from me from any connection to this person,
so that I might move on and learn in the process
whatever lessons I need to become a better person.'

Breathe on to the sigil the emotional energy you feel toward the person who harmed you.

'(Name of sigil) I release on to you this emotional energy which I have directed towards (name of person).'

Take the sigil and hold it over the censer. Set the sigil on fire, making sure to burn all of it. Repeat this process with every other sigil, if you have more than one.

Once all the sigils have been burned to ashes, take up the censer and walk to the edge of your home space, ideally to a road. Raise the censer high and say:

'I release (names of sigils) to Agave, to take this energy and disperse it from my life and return it to those from whom it came! May they learn whatever lessons are needed to make them better people. May I learn whatever lessons are needed to make me a better person.'

Take the censer back to your Nayati. Thank Agave for attending your majhahn and make him an offering.

Then conclude the majhahn in your usual manner.

After this majhahn, you should feel cleansed emotionally and no longer dwell on the individual who caused you harm. You've balanced the scales of justice for you and them. Be attentive to whatever learning situations enter into your life thereafter.

Alchemical
Transformation

In this stage of Pyralis training, the rehuna performs a series of majhahns that emulate the alchemical process of transformation. The rehuna should designate a room in their etheric Nayati that will be their alchemical laboratory and adorn this appropriately with symbolic items.

In ancient alchemy, the hermaphrodite, or rebis, was regarded as the fully-transformed and refined alchemist, who is in touch with all aspects of their being. Alchemical transformation involves use of the imagination, in the form of visualisations, meditations and dreams. As one 17th century alchemist wrote: 'Imagination is the star in man, celestial or super-celestial body' (from Ruland's *Lecixon Alchemiae* 1612).

The seven phases of alchemy are Calcination, Dissolution, Separation, Conjunction, Fermentation, Distillation, and Coagulation. Each is a stage in a process of refinement, designed to remove impurities – in this case within the being of the rehuna. The entire process involves the symbolic death and rebirth of the rehuna, designed to evolve them both psychically and spiritually. It concerns also the formation of the Sacred Androgyne within the psyche.

All stages of the work are undertaken by meditating on the

symbolism of each part of the process, with the intention that waking life will mirror the realisations, the transformation, thus affecting the rehuna on physical, mental and spiritual levels. This allows them to manifest the transformation in reality, in their own lives.

The rehuna embarking upon these alchemical workings should record all of their experiences, their thoughts, their dreams, and any symbolic events that occur in their lives during the period of transformation.

While there is no set time limit for each stage of the process, a period of no less than three days should be set aside for each. Should the rehuna wish, they may give each stage more time. There is also no set limit on how many majhahns or meditations should be performed for each stage. Some rehunas might feel it appropriate only to perform this work once; others might wish to spread the experience out over several sessions.

The Dehara of Alchemy

Prior to beginning work on this transformative process, the rehuna should meet with the Aghama in visualisation. The purpose of this is to ask him to introduce the rehuna to the Dehar of Alchemy. This Dehar has seven faces and seven forms, but ultimately these are all one entity. Each form represents a single stage of the alchemical process, and will serve as both initiator and guide. The seven dehara of alchemy are as follows:

Calcination: Areha

He has a muscular ebony body that emanates heat and wears an elaborate head-dress that is partly on fire. He generally wears a mask that covers his face, but when this is removed you see his face is scarred. His voice is rasping, barely more than a whisper, burned out by the fires contained within him.

Dissolution: Elolis

Elolis has blue skin, which is heavily decorated with white tattoos or paintings of swirling patterns. He generally appears in a bizarre costume similar to a jester or clown, which symbolises the alchemical step of dissolution. His voice contains a hint of sly humour.

Separation: Lhah

This dehar is coloured white on one side of his body and black on the other. He has markings of white on his black side and vice versa. He wears a two-coloured robe. His voice has a flowing aspect to it.

Conjunction: Voorhalis

Voorhalis has featureless face, but for a nose. He has no voice He symbolises the rehuna's unfinished state of being, and the hinted promise of becoming more. He is an aspect of the Sacred Androgyne, yet incomplete. His body might be perfect, but his senses are limited. He cannot see or hear, yet his nose guides him to the next stage of the work.

Fermentation: Dvelin

This dehar is coloured gold, but has blackened hands. His hands, representing the Putrefaction of this stage, eventually conduct the pure golden light of Fermentation into the rehuna. His attire similarly may be golden and beautiful, yet hemmed with rot. After Fermentation is complete, he becomes entirely golden. His voice is like music.

Distillation: Baloor

He has a blue face, but from that face extends the faces and aspects of all other alchemical dehara. He also has seven sets of arms, which represent the arms of all this dehar's aspects. His voice is many voices, incorporating those who have appeared previously in the work, including the silence of Voorhalis.

Coagulation: Phynyx

This dehar represents the phoenix of mythology, the creature that arises from its own bed of ashes. He is the purified version of the Sacred Androgyne, seen as a beautiful youth of radiating light. Within his voice is heard all the sounds of creation.

The Stages of Transformation

Calcination

Calcination is the process of being reduced by fire to ashes. This burns away constructions of the ego, illusory aspects of the psyche that the rehuna might create in order to shield themselves from harsh truths. Calcination's burn represents one of the greatest fears a rehuna can experience: overwhelming feelings of loss and failure. The ashes left by this conflagration being the process of awakening awareness, the realisation of the potential for growth.

For a week – or more – perform a majhahn to Areha. Ask him to initiate the process of calcination within you, where all that is obstructive to your evolution is reduced to ashes.

When you call upon this dehar to work with you, his lessons might be discomforting, such as forcing you to relive or recall incidents in your life that involve humiliation and embarrassment – the literal burning of the red face. Occurrences in your daily life might mirror events from the past, forcing you to confront them. Areha might take you to task harshly every day in your meditations.

During this work, you might experiences extremes of emotion and react hotly to situations. Observe what occurs without judgement. You should reflect upon events, and perceive in each one how self-protection mechanisms that have become habit might have sabotaged situations and opportunities in your life.

The first meditation you undertake in this state, should involve being burned by fire in the alchemical crucible. As to the setting of this meditation, you should let your imagination guide you. Calcination begins in Nevaath, the base sikra.

Dissolution

During this stage of the transformation the ashes of calcination are dissolved in water, so that remaining delusions and misconceptions are washed away.

Dissolution revolves around the idea of purification by water, of undesirable elements being washed away. It also represents the soume side of the psyche, the feminine, the deep mind.

Although the process of calcination burns away superficial self-preservation mechanisms, the rehuna might hold on tightly to untruths that prevent them facing fully the responsibility for their choices in life. In Dissolution the false constructions of the psyche continue be eroded, by the rehuna immersing themselves entirely in the unconscious mind. This takes control away from the conscious mind, so that buried thoughts and feelings are able to surface. At this point, the waters that have been kept in check gush forth, and while this can be a blissful experience, it can also be painful. The clearing purifies the energy within the body.

As with the previous stage, perform majhahns to Elolis, asking him to initiate the process of Dissolution and then act as your guide through it. He will highlight how any lies and excuses you might have created to make your life easier won't hold water during this stage. He will be inclined to mock you with the truth, demonstrating in a harsh but also humorous manner how easily you lie to yourself. Issues might come to the fore during this time when you are forced to confront untruths you've told yourself. From that moment you're able to review the situation and admit that part of the responsibility for whatever occurred in the past lies with you.

In contacting Elolis, you open the flood-gates within, allowing the purifying waters to pour through. During the meditations, you might feel as if you are deep underwater, and experience an irresistible pressure that shapes you. Dissolution continues the transformative process within the energy matrix of the body, and begins in the sacral sikra Ruuvaen

Separation

Separation is the process through which impurities are brought to the surface and removed. During this stage, it's common for the rehuna to feel a sense of separation from all that concerned them in previous stages of the process. This might bring to the surface insecurities they harbour concerning choices they've made in the past and where they are heading in life now.

Throughout this week, you should perform majhahns to Lhah, asking him to initiate the process of separation and then guide you through it. This stage promotes the rediscovery of dreams and visions that might have been rejected by the more ouana-aspected side of your being, which is concerned with the rational and empirical.

During this stage of the work, the material that separates from you can be regarded as dross that has clouded your mind and spirit; its removal allows clear, visionary sight.

Lhah might manifest in your dreams, a subconscious reminder of the process you are working through; a gentle, but insistent presence. He might offer you comfort. You may lay your head in his lap, when his hands gently reach into your being and pluck out the strings of energy that represent your fears. He encourages the release of self-imposed restrictions that might have limited your actions and options in life and whose removal enables you to experience your true nature.

This process begins in the solar plexus sikra, Iythra.

Conjunction

Conjunction recombines the refined elements remaining after Separation. It represents the realisation of the rehuna's true self, the union of soume and ouana aspects of the psyche, and initiates a more intuitive state of consciousness. Conjunction is the union of opposites, the combination of the conscious and unconscious minds, and the child of this union is the Rebis, the androgynous form freed from all restrictions and conditioning imposed by society's moral codes and belief systems, which can be overly harsh and imprisoning.

At this point, at the centre of the process, the rehuna must choose whether to continue with the process or return to their previous state of being. This is largely a symbolic choice, since the rehuna is unlikely to abandon their studies at this stage, but traditionally this is the point when the question is asked and the choice made.

For this stage of the process, call upon Voorhalis in majhahn and ask him to initiate Conjunction and thereafter be your guide through this stage. This process involves full assimilation of the hermaphroditic psyche – a harmonious conjunction of the soume and ouana – or male and female – aspects of being. This state combines intuition with logical thinking, and reflection with decision. The more instinctive aspects of your mind and spirit take on a sense of objective analysis; signs and omens might be read with greater acuity.

During this stage of the work, walk with Voorhalis. This can be done in reality and within the etheric realms simultaneously. Find a secluded place to walk where you won't be troubled by too many distractions. It might be that following the realisations and experiences of the previous stages, you feel in a mild state of shock and disorientation. A new self is being revealed, or rather a refined self. While walking, you are taking physical action but at the same time meditating, combining the physical with the non-physical.

This stage of the work can be viewed in one respect as a lull in the proceedings, the calm at the centre, when changes are accepted and absorbed. The process of Conjunction begins in the Heart sikra, Nyasava.

Fermentation

Fermentation has two parts, the first of which involves Putrefaction, or the death of the hermaphroditic child of Conjunction, followed by its rebirth at a higher level of being. The rehuna must submit to the Fermentation process, visualising this process of breaking down into putrid matter. Once this step is complete, the rays of the Aghama shine down and penetrate this matter, making it golden, bringing new life and regeneration.

In this sense Fermentation concerns renewed fertility, and Putrefaction can be seen as the process that provides the fertiliser for the fermenting process.

For this stage perform majhahns to Dvelin, asking him to initiate the process of Fermentation and to be your guide through it.

A majhahn should be performed in which you visualise yourself breaking down into waste matter. Then imagine the brightest golden light pouring down upon you, reconstituting your being into a better whole.

Putrefaction can be imagined as wallowing in the leftovers of your previous state of being, and from there accepting the challenge to transmute these fragments into something better. Dvelin appears within yellow light, bringing a sense of purification and growth. He encourages you to face the last deepest ingrained beliefs about yourself, to realise how unfounded they were, and to know you can grow from them.

This stage of the process offers the opportunity to discover and follow new paths, to acquire new skills or change the way you interact with others and the environment. It begins in the throat sikra, Raatha.

Distillation

Distillation in its literal sense means heating a liquid to the point of evaporation. The vapour from this process is then cooled and condensed, followed by the collection of the resulting distilled liquid. Distillation washes away remaining debris for the final stage of transformation. It represents the agitation of all components of being, to remove any remaining impurities, and the most difficult to remove insecurities and fears.

For this state of transformation, perform majhahns to Baloor, asking him to initiate the process of Distillation and to be your guide through it.

You should look upon this stage as the moment within the work when you distil your thoughts and emotions. This might involve shaking yourself free of sentimentality, even your own identity, in order to purify the unborn self – the being you are and can be.

Through majhahn, and by visualising this Distillation process within, focus upon raising the vibration of your personal agmara, the energy within. Visualise it rising from the lower sikras, up the centre of your body and into the higher sikras, into your physical brain. Here, see it solidifying into a radiant star of pure, crystalline light.

Distillation takes place in the third eye sikra, Ivlizaar.

Coagulation

Coagulation is the summation of the work, but also the beginning of more alchemical work. It is a higher transformation into a new being. In this stage, the rehuna becomes the Second Body of Golden Light, the refined Androgyne, a more advanced form than that of Conjunction.

For this final stage, call upon Phynyx, 'He Who Rises From Ashes'. Ask him to initiate Coagulation and to guide you through the process.

Visualise that the star you saw in Ivlizaar during Distillation now expands, its light radiating out into the crown sikra, Nimbara. Within this light, see the form of the Sacred Hermaphrodite take shape and emerge. Let this body of light merge with your own. This is the perfect being, free of impurities, refined and distilled.

In your everyday life, you should now begin to feel as if things are coming together – your view of your experiences should be more objective. While this doesn't mean your relationships and situations will be unrealistically perfect, you will be able to see your own influence in everything you experience, and how the 'coming together' of the knowledge you gained helps transform your reality in a physical way.

This alchemical transformation prepares you fully for the final stage of Pyralis, the descent into Xephelax.

Pyralis Ascension

Xephelax: the Dark Labyrinth

The rehuna comes now to the conclusion of their Pyralis training with the descent into the Dark Labyrinth.

Xephelax is a form of the underworld, which is found in the majority of spiritual systems. In Deharan lore it pertains particularly to caste ascension and training. It can be visualised as an immense labyrinth, otherlanes branching from it like fractals into other manifestations of the underworld or the lessons associated with it.

When the rehuna seeks to enter Xephelax from their etheric Nayati, they must first face and open the seven gates that bar the way to the heart of Xephelax beyond.

Ponclast: Dehar Demitto of Xephelax

Ponclast is the chesnari of Abrimel, and the Judge of Xephelax. He is found at its heart; the rehuna is led there in majhahn by Abrimel. The meeting with Ponclast is the Underworld Initiation, the true ascension to Pyralis, which leads to the transformative experiences of Algoma, the final caste of the Ulani tier.

When a rehuna undertakes the underworld journey, they are stripped of all illusions, including pride and honour. They are in a sense broken and then remade through the tribulations experienced in the underworld. Ponclast urges the rehuna to move past the condition of judgement towards acceptance. From there, they remake themselves through all they've learned. As such Ponclast is the presiding dehar of the Pyralisit caste

Ponclast is regarded as a dark character in Wraeththu lore. Once leader of the Varr tribe, infamous for dubious magical practices, he was vanquished by the 'enlightened' Gelaming and incarcerated in the forest of Gebaddon, a manifestation of Xephelax in mundane reality. He later escaped this prison to wreak more havoc, and during that time interacted with powerful yet amoral otherworld entities. Finally, Ponclast was subdued once more and exiled to a remote etheric realm.

In appearance, Ponclast is striking – tall, a little stooped, with long rags of black hair that fall nearly to the ground. He favours dressing in tattered robes of deepest crimson, and his arms may sometimes be visualised as entwined with black vines. His skin is like alabaster, yet his eyes are very dark. Like Abrimel, he lacks any aspect of nurturing and is impatient with weakness. A rehuna should face him with strength, and the conviction to command him.

The rehuna should meditate upon the Pyralis symbol for at least a week before undertaking the series of majhahns that comprise the Xephelax journey. They should fire walk to strengthen and cleanse themselves and, if necessary, revisit the Cloister of Abrimel for further purification. They should also converse with their aurago during meditation, and undertake etheric journeys with these guides, as further preparation for the Xephelax majhahn.

PONCLAST

Sikaara Work within Xephelax: Va-Sikra

Ponclast and Abrimel are associated with Xephelax, journeys through it, and also with the underworld aspects of the sikra energy centres, which are represented by seven energy gates. The rehuna works with Abrimel to connect with each sikra for the underworld journey. They will follow the trail that the sikras represent to the heart of Xephelax and Ponclast. The sikras correspond in location to those of the Sikaara system, but are regarded as the 'reverse' or 'dark' versions of them and are known as va-sikra, the term deriving from Ponclast's original tribe, the Varrs.

Mal is the first va-sikra, dark, intense red in colour. It may be activated via grissecon (or aruna magic) and enables a release from attachment to the physical world.

Aurith is the orange of burning embers, and centres around the concept of fear.

Saal is associated with pride and is dazzling gold in colour.

Alik focuses upon the passions of love and hate in their extreme forms. It is an intense, dark green, shifting with shadows.

Azul, a dull blue, is associated with shame.

Iskara, which is purple, reveals all subtle judgements.

Malith, without colour, focuses upon emptiness and spaciousness.

Before performing the Xephelax majhahns, the rehuna should devise six symbols or objects that he will give to Abrimel, representing respectively their fear, pride, passions, shame, and judgements.

Descent into Xephelax

The Xephelax journey should be performed over seven consecutive sessions. The rehuna may choose their own timetable for this, judging for themselves when they have assimilated the knowledge of each chamber of the descent, but generally leaving no more than a week between each journey.

Should a rehuna feel they are not ready to pass to the next chamber after a week, (at any time during this series of majhahns), they should revisit the Cloisters of Abrimel to address any blockages or fears that may be holding them back. They could also speak with their aurago in meditation for guidance. Then they should begin the series of majhahns again from the beginning.

A rehuna should not take their aurago with them during the Xephelax majhahns, as it's important they experience each chamber of the underworld alone. But if the aurago should appear spontaneously and naturally within any part of the majhahn then the rehuna should accept their presence and not try to dismiss them.

The instructions for these majhahns allow plenty of space for the rehuna to visualise more details within the individual chambers of Xephelax. There is adequate time within the journeys for the rehuna to meditate at the centre of each chamber, examining its qualities and seeing reflections of these qualities within themselves. Rehunas might meet entities within the chambers, or have other images or byways come to them they wish to explore. The only constraint is that the rehuna should not venture beyond the farthest gate that has not yet been opened for them. Each chamber should have one session devoted to it, and no more than one new chamber should be explored within each majhahn. This is to ensure

111

that the knowledge from each chamber is fully assimilated and examined. The Descent into Xephelax is not a journey that should be rushed through.

One: The Road to Xephelax, the Gate of Mal and the Chamber of Aurith

Construct your etheric Nayati, enter it, and prepare for majhahn. Evoke whichever dehara feel appropriate to you to watch over your body as you travel within the etheric realms. Compose yourself within the centre of your Nayati and perform the breathing exercises you learned during Acantha training. When you are ready, focus your intention and call upon Abrimel. (You may devise an invocation in your own words, or use the following example):

'Astale, Abrimel, Guide to the Ways Below,
I summon you here to lead me to the gates of Xephelax,
the realm whose paths you know.
I will pass through the gates without ally.
I will cast the adornments and armours of the mundane world aside.
Abrimel, chesnari of Ponclast, the Dark Hostling, you are the sentinel of perilous paths.
Know that I undertake this journey to enter the Labyrinth of my own free will and with the strength of Pyralis within me. '

Draw the symbol of Pyralis in the air before you, visualising it as flame. Intend that this portal will take you to the realm known as The Road to Xephelax. Step through the symbol into the realm beyond.

The Road to Xephelax is a stark and barren realm. Ahead, you see an unimaginably gigantic range of spiky black mountains. The first gate lies at their feet. The sky is red above you and a dull, dark crimson sun hangs low within it; the sun is immense, but gives no heat. There seems to be no life within this realm.

When you reach the foot of the mountains, the sun is now

hidden by them, and blackness covers the land. You can discern a chasm in the rock ahead of you, darker than its surroundings. As you approach, the sheer walls of obsidian seem to engulf you, but after you have walked for a short way, your eyes adjust and you can perceive some detail of your surroundings. You see that the path you are walking curves before you, and you realise you are following a spiral. Even though you can see this much, there is no light – when you look up between the rocks the sky is matte black, with no moon or stars.

Presently, you reach a wall, which seems impassable. Then you realise that a dark figure stands before it, robed in dark colours. Its head is covered by a hood, which it now throws back to reveal itself as Abrimel.

You say: 'Astale, Abrimel, Sentinel of the Ways Below. I ask you to open the Gate of Mal that I might pass through.'

Abrimel responds. 'Mal is opened by aruna without body, without mind. It opens at the ignition of a star.'

'Then call forth the essence of your chesnari, Ponclast, so you may open the Gate of Mal.'

You see a shadowy form manifest before you, which is the essence of Ponclast, or the representation of his arunic connection with Abrimel. This being steps forth from the darkness, and melds with Abrimel. This is no simple aruna, nor a representation of love. It is the conjunction of two beings of energy, on all levels, that in their union create the spark that reveals the Gate of Mal.

You see this portal before you, immense and dark red, cut into the rock. You know that you must leave all sense of sexual identity at this gate and walk through free of its trappings.

When you pass through the Gate of Mal, you find yourself in very different surroundings. You are in a cavern of dull flames, with pools of lava to either side of the path that are almost black, shot with dark crimson crevices. This is the chamber of Aurith. The walls are of volcanic rock and the air smells of burning. You can hear strange cracking and groaning noises, and the lava churns as if something is attempting to rise and break through its surface. As you walk on, to the other side of the cavern, you become aware of fear rising within you. You feel threatened, as if your very survival is at stake. Your heartbeat increases. You want to run.

Call upon the strength of Pyralis to keep your steps even, to calm your heart.

Spend some time in the centre of the Chamber of Aurith, and contemplate what its properties mean to you personally. Here you may externalise symbols of your fears and examine them objectively. In this realm you may remain detached from them and they cannot overwhelm you.

When you are ready to move on, continue your journey across the vast chamber until you reach another wall of solid obsidian. Say

'Astale, Abrimel, Sentinel of the Ways Below, I ask you to come to me now. Open the Gate of Aurith that I might pass through.'

Abrimel hears your request and appears before the rock wall. He says: 'You must relinquish terror to open the Gate of Aurith. Give it to me.'

You hand Abrimel the symbol of your fears. 'Take my terror. Open the Gate of Aurith that I may pass through it at any time.'

Once you have handed Abrimel the symbol, you feel somehow lighter, freer. All your fears have left you. Whatever you might face, you will do so with calm detachment.

Abrimel puts his hand upon the obsidian wall and a vast gateway appears; molten lines within the rock.

Say: 'I thank you, Abrimel, for opening the Gate of Aurith for me. When we meet again, I will pass through it into Saal.'

Now return to normal consciousness and conclude your majhahn in your usual manner.

Afterwards, write up notes of all you can remember of your majhahn.

Two: The Chamber of Saal

Begin your majhahn as before, making the journey along the Road to Xephelax and the Gate of Mal. When you reach this gate it is now open, and you can walk through it into the chamber of Aurith. While the physical features of this chamber still remain, they now feel only like pictures to you: you have absorbed the knowledge from Aurith. As you cross this chamber, visualise that any vestiges of its qualities, which you might have brought with you from your reality, are absorbed by your surroundings. You experience the same feeling of freedom as you did the first time you visited this chamber.

Pass to the far side of the chamber, where you see Abrimel standing beside the Gate of Aurith. The gate still glows with molten fiery lines within the rock.

Say: 'Astale, Abrimel, Sentinel of the Ways Below. I am here to pass through the Gate of Aurith to the Chamber of Saal, on my way to the heart of Xephelax.'

Abrimel inclines his head to you and with one hand pushes open the great gate.

You pass into the chamber of Saal, where the walls are of gold, shining with a dazzling light that almost blinds you. Here, at once, you become aware of pride, the things you believe set you above all others. Perhaps you take pride in being honourable and strong. Even those with the lowest opinion of themselves take pride in their victimhood and wear it as a medal of valour. Whatever form pride takes within you, now it manifests for you to observe.

Walk to the centre of the chamber, your head held high. Here, spend some time contemplating the qualities of Saal and how they are mirrored within you. Examine the manifestations of pride within you, but without judgement.

When you are ready to proceed, cross to the far side of the chamber, where you come again to an impenetrable wall.

Say 'Astale, Abrimel, Sentinel of the Ways Below. I ask you to come to me now, and open the Gate of Saal that I might pass through.'

Abrimel responds to your request and manifests before the gate. He says, 'You must relinquish pride to open the Gate of Saal. Give it to me.'

You hand Abrimel the symbol of your pride. 'Take my pride. Open the Gate of Saal.'

Once Abrimel has taken the symbol, you feel the sense of pride disappear entirely, and again you feel lighter and freer. You realise that the qualities you are relinquishing are a burden. Sometimes, they might be necessary in life, and you should not judge yourself for them, but in this realm, it's possible to lay them aside and experience the pure, unencumbered core of your being.

Abrimel puts his hand upon the obsidian wall and the vast gateway appears; blazing golden lines within the rock.

Say: 'I thank you, Abrimel, for opening the Gate of Saal for me. When we meet again, I will pass through it into Alik.'

Now return to normal consciousness and conclude your majhahn in your usual manner.

Afterwards, write up notes of all you can remember of your majhahn.

Three: The Chamber of Alik

Begin as you did previously, making your way through the Gate of Mal, and across the chambers of Aurith and Saal. As you walk through the chambers, release any vestiges of their qualities you might have brought with you from mundane reality. Experience the same sense of freedom you felt on your previous visit to this place.

Pass to the far side of the Chamber of Saal, where you see Abrimel standing beside the Gate of Alik. The gate still glows with blazing golden lines within the rock.

Say: 'Astale, Abrimel, Sentinel of the Ways Below. I am here to pass through the Gate of Saal to the Chamber of Alik, on my way to the heart of Xephelax.'

Abrimel inclines his head to you and with one hand pushes open the great gate.

You now find yourself in the cavern of Alik. The walls here are green like serpentine and running with water. There are dim torches of greenish flame to light your way. Pools to either side of the path and murky and swampy. This is the chamber of roiling passions, the dark fires of love and hate, and its shadows, jealousy, paranoia, possessiveness, obsession, envy, intolerance. Love without compassion. Hate without reason. You experience these churning feelings as you cross the cavern floor.

In the centre of the chamber, once again contemplate the qualities of this place and how they mirror aspects of yourself. Meditate upon these facets without judgement or attachment, and when you feel ready, move on.

As before, you reach an impenetrable wall. You say:

'Astale, Abrimel, Sentinel of the Ways Below. I ask you to come to me now and open the Gate of Alik that I might pass through.'

Abrimel responds to your request and appears before the gate. He says: 'You must relinquish passion to open the Gate of Alik. Give it to me.'

You hand Abrimel the appropriate symbol. 'Take my love and my hate and all volatile passions. Open the Gate of Alik.'

As before, you feel you are growing lighter once the symbol has been relinquished. Abrimel touches the wall and the gate materialises within the stone, its carvings running with water.

Say: 'I thank you, Abrimel, for opening the Gate of Alik for me. When we meet again, I will pass through it into Azul.'

Now return to normal consciousness and conclude your majhahn in your usual manner.

Afterwards, write up notes of all you can remember of your majhahn.

Four: The Chamber of Azul

Begin as you did previously, making your way through the Gate of Mal, and across the chambers of Aurith, Saal and Alik. As you walk through the chambers, release any vestiges of their qualities you might have brought with you from mundane reality. Experience the same sense of freedom you felt on your last visit to this place.

Pass to the far side of the Chamber of Alik, where you see Abrimel standing beside the gate, which is still visible within the rock. The gate runs with narrow streams of water that follow lines within the rock.

Say: 'Astale, Abrimel, Sentinel of the Ways Below. I am here to pass through the Gate of Alik to the Chamber of Azul, on my way to the heart of Xephelax.'

Abrimel inclines his head to you and with one hand pushes open the great gate.

Now you step into the cavern of Azul, where the walls are of a dull blue stone that does not shine. There is only rubble around you, and the air feels oppressive. Here, you become aware of shame and all that you learned of it in the Cloister of Abrimel. You experience again the leaden burden of it, but now you're able to do so objectively.

Spend time in the centre of the Chamber of Azul contemplating the qualities of this place and its reflections within you.

When you are ready to move on, cross the chamber to its farthest side. Here you reach an impenetrable wall of dull blue stone. You say:

'Astale, Abrimel, Sentinel of the Ways Below. I ask you to

come to me now and open the Gate of Azul that I might pass through.'

Abrimel responds to your request and appears before the gate. He says: 'You must relinquish shame to open the Gate of Azul. Give it to me.'

You hand Abrimel the appropriate symbol. 'Take my shame. Open the Gate of Azul.'

As before, you feel you are growing lighter, free of shame, once the symbol has been relinquished. Abrimel touches the wall and the blue stone cracks and crumbles, revealing the gate within it, which glows with lines of faint azure light.

Say: 'I thank you, Abrimel, for opening the Gate of Azul for me. When we meet again, I will pass through it into Iskara.'

Now return to normal consciousness and conclude your majhahn in your usual manner.

Afterwards, write up notes of all you can remember of your majhahn.

Five: The Chamber of Iskara

Begin as you did previously, making your way through the Gate of Mal, and across the chambers of Aurith, Saal, Alik and Azul. As you walk through the chambers, release any vestiges of their qualities you might have brought with you from mundane reality. Experience the same sense of freedom you felt on your last visit to this place.

Pass to the far side of the Chamber of Azul, where you see Abrimel standing beside the gate, which is still visible within the rock. The gate glows with faint blue lines.

Say: 'Astale, Abrimel, Sentinel of the Ways Below. I am here to pass through the Gate of Azul to the Chamber of Iskara, on my way to the heart of Xephelax.'

Abrimel inclines his head to you and with one hand pushes open the great gate.

Now you find yourself in the cavern of Iskara, which is constructed of dark purple stone. There are glints within this rock that looks like eyes. Here is the chamber of subtle judgments, upon and by you. You realise that judgements are conclusions that prevent further query. To judge a matter is to end it, limit your own thinking.

As within the other chambers, spend some time in this place contemplating its qualities and how they manifest within your own life. When you are ready to move on, cross the chamber to its farthest wall, which is made of dark purple stone.

Say: 'Astale, Abrimel, Sentinel of the Ways Below. I ask you to come to me now and open the Gate of Iskara that I might pass through.'

Abrimel appears before the gate and says: 'You must relinquish judgement to open the Gate of Iskara. Give it to me.'

You hand Abrimel a symbol. 'Take my judgement. Open the Gate of Iskara.'

Once Abrimel has taken the symbol, you become aware of being free of all judgement, and feel lighter in your being. Abrimel touches the wall and reveals the gate within it, which is shot with glowing purple lines.

Say: 'I thank you, Abrimel, for opening the Gate of Iskara for me. When we meet again, I will pass through it into Malith.'

Now return to normal consciousness and conclude your majhahn in your usual manner.

Afterwards, write up notes of all you can remember of your majhahn.

Six: The Chamber of Malith

Begin as you did previously, making your way through the Gate of Mal, and across the chambers of Aurith, Saal, Alik, Azul and Iskara. As you walk through the chambers, release any vestiges of their qualities you might have brought with you from mundane reality. Experience the same sense of freedom you felt on your last visit to this place.

Pass to the far side of the Chamber of Iskara, where you see Abrimel standing beside the gate, which is still visible within the rock. The gate glows with patterns of purple light.

Say: 'Astale, Abrimel, Sentinel of the Ways Below. I am here to pass through the Gate of Iskara to the Chamber of Malith, on my way to the heart of Xephelax.'

Abrimel inclines his head to you and with one hand pushes open the great gate.

Beyond the gate lies the final chamber of Malith. Light and free as you now feel, it isn't shocking or unsettling when you realise you are hanging in a void. Malith is emptiness and spaciousness, the place that exists beyond all negative thoughts and feelings that bind a soul and limits it.

This is a place of peace and contemplation and while it is the gateway to the heart of Xephelax and the Throne of Ponclast, it also connects with Nimbara, the seat of consciousness in Sikaara. Spend some time in this place, contemplating the endless tranquillity beyond all restrictive emotions and drives. Experience pure consciousness.

From here also, you can access other aspects and realms of the underworld. Be aware you might conjure portals to these places should you wish, but such journeys are not for this particular majhahn.

When you are ready, call upon Abrimel:

Say: 'Astale, Abrimel, Sentinel of the Ways Below. I ask you to come to me now and open the Gate of Malith that I might pass through.'

Abrimel appears before the gate and says: 'There is no cost to this passage but that of a free heart and mind. You have cast off all restraints. Put your hand with mine to open the Gate to the Heart of Xephelax.'

Abrimel raises a hand and you do so too, so that your palms touch. This connection conjures a pulse of indigo light. As you pull your hands apart, so a portal of glowing indigo radiance unfolds between you, which is the gate to the Heart of Xephelax.

Bow to Abrimel and say, 'I thank you, Abrimel, Sentinel of the Ways, for opening with me the Gate of Malith. When next we meet I will enter the Heart of Xephelax.'

Now return to normal consciousness and conclude your majhahn in your usual manner.

Afterwards, write up notes of all you can remember of your majhahn.

Seven: The Heart of Xephelax

Begin as you did previously, making your way through the Gate of Mal, and across the chambers of Aurith, Saal, Alik, Azul and Iskara. As you walk through the chambers, release any vestiges of their qualities you might have brought with you from mundane reality. Experience the same sense of freedom you felt on your last visit to this place.

Pass into Malith, where you see Abrimel beside the portal, which pulses with indigo light.

Say: 'Astale, Abrimel, Sentinel of the Ways Below. I am here to pass through the Gate of Malith to the heart of Xephelax. Walk with me to the Throne of the Dark Hostling, Ponclast, your chesnari.'

Abrimel inclines his head and reaches out to you with one hand. You take hold of this and pass with Abrimel through the portal.

The final stages of this journey and its imagery are personal to you; therefore you are provided with no detailed descriptions of imagery and events to lead you. Your guides are Abrimel and your own imagination, your own knowledge, your own aspirations.

Know that you walk with Abrimel to the dehar of the Underworld, and that in meeting Ponclast, he will initiate you as Pyralisit, so you may enter the final caste of this tier of study: Algoma.

Visualise the Heart of Xephelax as you will. Pass ultimately to the Throne of Ponclast and tell him of your will to ascend to Pyralis. Let the initiation proceed as it manifests within your imagination, but part of the procedure will involve Ponclast attuning you to the symbol of Pyralis, through his breath, gaze, hands, or through aruna.

Experience fully the sense of ascension. At its conclusion, you will pass from the fires of Pyralis into Algoma, the Valley of Flowers and the place of transformations.

Once the initiation is complete and Ponclast advises you it is time to depart, visualise a portal of white light appearing beside you. This is your gateway to Nimbara.

Step through the portal into your own body, into the seventh sikra. From here, reorient yourself into mundane reality and return to normal consciousness. Conclude the majhahn in your usual manner and write up notes of your experiences.

Algoma

The Path of the Algomalid

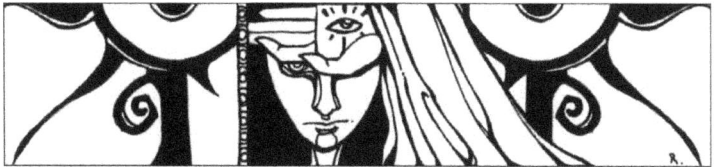

Algoma is the Valley of Flowers. After the trials and deep initiations of Acantha and Pyralis, this is the caste of Transformation.

Attaining the ascension of Algoma grants the rank of hienama, an intermediate teacher, who may train rehunas and conduct ascension majhahns up to their own level within the system. They may create other hienamas, but not above Algoma level. Some examples of initiation/caste ascension majhahns will be given in the appendices to this book.

For a rehuna to take on the mantle of hienama, and offer spiritual teaching in the Deharan system, they must undergo the final initiation into Algoma. By this stage, the rehuna should be aware of their whole being and how they function. It should be understood that no rehuna can be a perfect being, entirely free of all adverse traits and tendencies that are part of incarnation in the material world. Rather, they should simply be *aware* of these tendencies in themselves and others, thus making them more tolerant and forgiving. This does not mean they should feel obliged to train or work with any individual with whom the hienama feels that progress cannot be made – at least through their personal teaching. Tolerance does not include enduring situations and relationships that are in effect deleterious to one's own well-being. One individual's ideal teacher might not be ideal for another. Understanding of Algoma's lessons aids the hienama in identifying such situations, and also when a student has learned all they can and must individuate, or seek their next teacher.

As well as being teachers, hienamas are also traditionally called upon to conduct rites of passage, such as bondings, funeral rites, namings and other significant rituals of life.

The Symbol Algoma

The third symbol of the Ulani tier represents inner transformation – a flowering. The thorny pathways and the purifying fires of the previous castes have been faced and conquered. What lies ahead is the preparation for entering the gateway to the final tier of Deharan Magic: Nahir Nuri.

Algoma is drawn by beginning at the tail and working up and through the spiral, an archetypal symbol of the sacred. The double helix, or lemniscate, is added last. The symbol may be visualised as three dimensional, with the tail being closest to the eye. The lemniscate can be visualised as being beyond the head of the spiral.

In majhahn, Algoma is a transformative energy that can be used to empower goals and effect healing, especially of a mental or spiritual nature.

Meditation upon Algoma

The spiral of Algoma mirrors the journey of Xephelax, reminding the rehuna of the lessons they recently learned, but at the heart of this symbol lies the double helix, representative of higher learning and knowledge, the gateway to the more cosmic experiences of Nahir Nuri. It can be seen, in a way, as the portal to the stars.

The lemniscate here represents the rehuna's ultimate potential, and is the vessel of their voyage of discovery. The majhahns and exercises of Algoma are in nature gentler than those of the previous tiers.

Before embarking upon the majhahns of Algoma, the rehuna should meditate upon the symbol. Given below is one example of how this might be approached.

The Blossoming Light

Visualise the symbol of Algoma before you. See it enlarging, radiating glittering beams of light that appear to emanate from its heart. The light falls upon you, is absorbed by your body, and enlivens your sikras. See within this radiance, a multitude of blooms forming and opening, exploding into stars of light, only to be replaced by more, like a fractal pattern. This is the eternal flowering, the constant ignition of thought and ideas, of emotion and creative impulses that exists within us all. Algoma vitalises all these faculties and traits. Feel that restorative energy flowing through and around you.

Imagine the symbol becomes so huge you can walk upon it as a spiralling pathway of light. Follow the path to its heart and then step into the lemniscate. Beyond you find the realm of Algoma, the Valley of Flowers. It can be a garden or a wild landscape. Within it are all the visualised temples and cities of those who have travelled here before.

Explore this realm and observe what initial ideas and impulses come to you concerning this new tier of your training. You may meet entities who will be with you during this process, or with whom you can work to form fully-realised dehara demitto. You may also have ideas for particular new majhahns with which you wish to experiment. Algoma is a realm of ideas and changes, with limitless potential and no boundaries.

Merging with the Dehara

An aspect of Algoma transformation is merging with the dehara themselves. The rehuna views themselves through the eyes of the dehara.

For all these majhahns, the rehuna should construct their etheric Nayati in their preferred manner, invoking whatever entities they feel appropriate to protect and watch over them while they conduct their visualisations.

The majhahns of merging may be performed in an order of the rehuna's choice, but are presented here beginning with Miyacala.

The format of these majhahns is first to construct an etheric self, enter into it, and then generate a manifestation of the appropriate dehar. Once these two forms have been created, the rehuna absorbs the essence of the dehar into themselves, and then walks with deharan awareness, visiting the temple of their chosen dehar. Finally, the rehuna deconstructs the etheric forms and returns to normal consciousness.

MIYACALA

Merging with Miyacala

Etheric Self Generation

Allow awareness of your physical body to fade. Dissolve into a body of light, without form, and visualise yourself breathing as one with the ethers.

Now generate an image of yourself, sitting cross-legged, and floating above the surface of a limitless ocean of white mist, beneath an endless milky sky. Imagine this location as immensely vast – stretch its horizons – symbolising your mind at its widest.

Focus upon your breathing and become an embodiment of tranquillity. Let all mundane concerns disappear. Observe the details of your body, adornments and posture, and enter into this self-generated construct.

Miyacala Generation

Visualise that floating before you, just above the surface of the mist, is a large, white aganymphna bloom that is big enough to sit on. As you gaze at this flower, its petals open gradually to reveal its centre, which is faintly yellow. Above it, at the level of your heart, is a small glowing white shape. This is the symbol of Miyacala.

As you focus upon the symbol, it begins to vibrate and become surrounded by light. This shining radiance expands, until the symbol becomes absorbed within it. The light fills your view. It begins to emit brilliant silver sparks that spiral out like fireworks. Eventually, this light coalesces above the heart of the flower and takes on shape.

Miyacala is seated before you. He is pale-skinned and dressed in white. His eyes are milky blind and he has a star upon his forehead to represent his keen inner sight. He sits cross-legged upon the centre of the aganymphna, surrounded by its enfolding petals that glow with soft silver light.

Miyacala appears serene, but you are conscious of his great power. You are aware of his keen sight, his ability to penetrate to the truth of any matter, to find solutions to every dilemma. He is the embodiment of creative thought, the essence of transformation through the direction of will in magic. He merely thinks something to make it so, and in this way he also represents majhahn free of all trappings and props; the seed of thought and desire and will that is the true agency of achieving effects. His left hand is raised, the palm displayed to you. Here too is a star. He sees right into you, to your deepest secrets. Nothing can be concealed from him. When you stand before him, you do so naked of all artifice.

Change your perception now, move your awareness into Miyacala. Look out though his eyes. Regard your own form through his gaze. See within you the power to manifest positive change in your life, to create solutions and plans and ideas. See within you the ability to perceive truth, no matter how many layers of untruth are put over it. This includes the truths within yourself, and is part of Miyacala within you.

Absorption of Miyacala

Now allow your perception to shift again, back into your etheric body. The form of Miyacala dissolves, becomes again white light, representative of his power, strength and clarity, the power to change reality through the expression of thought, the manifestation of ideas.

Breathe in the white light, so that Miyacala becomes part of you, absorbed into your being. Now you look from your own eyes with his vision.

Miyacala s Temple

Walk now, with Miyacala's sight, to the Nayati of Tahanica, Miyacala's temple. Take in details of the path and the approach to the Nayati. You will see the symbol of Tahanica.

This is both the symbol of the Nayati and of the flow of its etheric energy. It can be used to augment magical workings with the energy of Miyacala's attributes. It may also be used as a ward, a symbol of protection that invokes Miyacala's clear sight and the banishment of untruth.

Enter Tahanica and explore its chambers. Find a place that feels right to you and here sit down. Focus upon the symbol of Tahanica and absorb it into yourself. Observe the rays of your own power as the force that can manifest your desires into being. Accept your own power as a lightning force to achieve your aims.

Conclusion of the Majhahn

When you are ready to conclude the majhahn, and return to the aganymphna flower. Here, sit down again, and allow your generated body to dissolve. Breathe in the body of light and allow it to energise you. Become conscious gradually of your physical body in your earthly Nayati and end the majhahn in your usual manner.

AGAVE

Merging with Agave

Etheric Self Generation

Allow awareness of your physical body to fade. Dissolve into a body of light, without form, and visualise yourself breathing as one with the ethers.

Now generate an image of yourself, sitting cross-legged, and floating above the surface of a limitless sea of flame, beneath a red sky like a sunset. The flame cannot burn you, but is simply a representation of Agave's traits. Imagine this location as immensely vast – stretch its horizons – symbolising your mind at its widest.

Focus upon your breathing and become an embodiment of tranquillity. Let all mundane concerns disappear. Observe the details of your body, adornments and posture, and enter into this self-generated construct.

Agave Generation

Visualise that floating before you, just above the surface of the sea of fire, is a large, deep red aganymphna bloom that is big enough to sit on. As you gaze at this flower, its petals open gradually to reveal its centre, which glows bright orange. Above it, at the level of your heart, is a small glowing orange shape. This is the symbol of Agave.

As you focus upon the symbol, it begins to vibrate and becomes surrounded by light. This shining radiance expands, until the symbol becomes absorbed within it. The light fills your view. It begins to emit brilliant red and orange sparks that spiral out like fireworks. Eventually, this light coalesces above the heart of the flower and takes on shape.

Agave is seated before you. His skin is golden and his hair is like liquid flame. He sits cross-legged at the heart of the aganymphna, surrounded by the petals that are like flames themselves. Agave appears serene, but you are conscious of the power smouldering within him, his ability to purge and cleanse, his will that you use to empower all majhahns. He wears only a pair of scarlet embroidered trousers. In his left hand, he holds a flaming knife, to represent the cutting away of outmoded behaviours and ideas, to give space for the new to grow. Be aware that from him nothing is concealed.

Change your perception now, move your awareness into Agave. Look out though his eyes. Regard your own form through his gaze. See within you the power of your own will, which fires your magical endeavours. See the electrical fire of creativity that allows you to manifest ideas into reality and the ability within you to effect change through magical action. All of these are traits of Agave within you.

Absorption of Agave

Now allow your perception to shift again, back into your etheric body. The form of Agave dissolves, becomes again fiery light, representative of his power, strength and passion, the power to make change.

Breathe in the orange-red light, so that Agave becomes part of you, absorbed into your being. Now you look from your own eyes with his vision.

The Temple of Agave

Walk now, with Agave's sight, to the Nayati of Igniteran, Agave's temple. Take in details of the path and the approach to the Nayati. You will see the symbol of Igniteran.

This is both the symbol of the Nayati and of the flow of its etheric energy. It can be used to augment magical workings with the energy of Agave's attributes. It may also be used as a ward, a symbol of protection that invokes fiery sword and the will to repel harm.

Enter Igniteran and explore its chambers. Find a place that feels right to you and here sit down. Focus upon the symbol of Igniteran and absorb it into yourself. Observe the power of your own will and vitality as a force that can manifest your desires into being, that can move obstacles and that can also protect. Accept your own power as a brilliant fire that helps you achieve your aims.

Conclusion of the Majhahn

When you are ready to conclude the majhahn, and return to the aganymphna flower. Here, sit down again, and allow your generated body to dissolve. Breathe in the body of light and allow it to energise you. Become conscious gradually of your physical body in your earthly Nayati and end the majhahn in your usual manner.

LUNIL

Merging with Lunil

Etheric Self Generation

Allow awareness of your physical body to fade. Dissolve into a body of light, without form, and visualise yourself breathing as one with the ethers.

Now generate an image of yourself, sitting cross-legged, and floating above the surface of a limitless tranquil ocean, beneath an endless cerulean blue sky. Imagine this location as immensely vast – stretch its horizons – symbolising your mind at its widest.

Focus upon your breathing and become an embodiment of tranquillity. Let all mundane concerns disappear. Observe the details of your body, adornments and posture, and enter into this self-generated construct.

Lunil Generation

Visualise that floating before you, just above the surface of the sea of fire, is a large, aquamarine aganymphna bloom that is big enough to sit on. As you gaze at this flower, its petals open gradually to reveal its centre, which glows a deep rich blue. Above it, at the level of your heart, is a small glowing azure shape. This is the symbol of Lunil.

As you focus upon the symbol, it begins to vibrate and becomes surrounded by light. This shining radiance expands, until the symbol becomes absorbed within it. The light fills your view. It begins to emit brilliant blue sparks – cobalt, turquoise, azure – that spiral out like fireworks. Eventually, this light coalesces above the heart of the flower and takes on shape.

Lunil is seated before you, in his aspect of magical power. His skin is of a blue shade, and his hair is like liquid around him, strung with pearls and water weed. He sits cross-legged at the heart of the aganymphna, surrounded by the shining blue petals that are beaded with moisture. He appears serene, but you are conscious of his power, his ability to grant the sight of intuition and magic, his ability to erode, through steadily flowing power, all obstacles to contentment. He wears only a pair of blue-green embroidered trousers, which are decorated with seed pearls. His body is adorned with ropes of pearls. In his left hand, he holds a blade of glowing blue-white crystal that represents the power of magic. Be aware that from him nothing is concealed.

Change your perception now, move your awareness into Lunil. Look out though his eyes. Regard your own form through his gaze. See within you the power of your own instincts and intuition, which informs your magical endeavours. See the flowing waves of gentle but inexorable force that allow you to create change, to express yourself, and also to heal. All of these are traits of Lunil within you.

Absorption of Lunil

Now allow your perception to shift again, back into your etheric body. The form of Lunil dissolves, becomes again pulsing blue light, representative of his power, strength and wisdom, the power of imagination.

Breathe in the blue light, so that Lunil becomes part of you, absorbed into your being. Now you look from your own eyes with his vision.

The Temple of Lunil

Walk now, with Lunil's sight, to the Nayati of Loraylah, Lunil's temple. Take in details of the path and the approach to the Nayati. You will see the symbol of Loraylah.

This is both the symbol of the Nayati and of the flow of its etheric energy. It can be used to augment magical workings with the energy of Lunil's attributes. It may also be used as a symbol of healing that invokes Lunil's soothing waters, as well as deep love and compassion.

Enter Loraylah and explore its chambers. Find a place that feels right to you and here sit down. Focus upon the symbol of Loraylah and absorb it into yourself. Observe your own intuition and compassion as a force that can strengthen and temper your magical desires, a force that can also heal and cleanse. See the tide of your intentions being able to erode and remove all obstacles in your path, all negative situations that impede you. Accept your own power as the inexorable force that can help you achieve your aims and desires, and as a strongly-flowing river that helps you to work wisely.

Conclusion of the Majhahn

When you are ready to conclude the majhahn, and return to the aganymphna flower. Here, sit down again, and allow your generated body to dissolve. Breathe in the body of light and allow it to energise you. Become conscious gradually of your physical body in your earthly Nayati and end the majhahn in your usual manner.

Merging with Aruhani

Etheric Self Generation

Allow awareness of your physical body to fade. Dissolve into a body of light, without form, and visualise yourself breathing as one with the ethers.

Now generate an image of yourself, sitting cross-legged, and floating above the surface of a limitless grassy plain, beneath an endless sky. Imagine this location as immensely vast – stretch its horizons – symbolising your mind at its widest.

Focus upon your breathing and become an embodiment of tranquillity. Let all mundane concerns disappear. Observe the details of your body, adornments and posture, and enter into this self-generated construct.

Aruhani Generation

Visualise that floating before you, just above the surface of the plain, is a large, deep green aganymphna bloom that is big enough to sit on. As you gaze at this flower, its petals open gradually to reveal its centre, which glows a deep yellow. Above it, at the level of your heart, is a small glowing emerald shape. This is the symbol of Aruhani.

As you focus upon the symbol, it begins to vibrate and becomes surrounded by light. This shining radiance expands, until the symbol becomes absorbed within it. The light fills your view. It begins to emit brilliant green sparks – viridian, moss green, jade and lime – that spiral out like fireworks. Eventually, this light coalesces above the heart of the flower and takes on shape.

Aruhani is seated before you. His appearance is serene and calm, yet you're aware of his power as both creator and destroyer. He is black-skinned, with a multitude of long black braids that are twisted with ropes of dark green gem-stones. He is draped in sumptuous fabrics of various shades of green, deep gold and earthy brown, and adorned with precious jewels. In his left hand, he holds a living branch that holds bud, flower and fruit to represent the past present and future. Be aware that from him nothing is concealed.

Change your perception now, move your awareness into Aruhani. Look out though his eyes. Regard your own form through his gaze. Accept yourself as you are; not perfect, but a mass of aspects, which sometimes might conflict. You can create and you can destroy, but you should do so with awareness. All of these are traits of Aruhani within you.

Absorption of Aruhani

Now allow your perception to shift again, back into your etheric body. The form of Aruhani dissolves, becomes again radiant green light of many hues, representative of his power of creation, his vigour and sexual potency as both hostling and sire, his wisdom, his objective discernment free of clouding emotion.

Breathe in the green light, so that Aruhani becomes part of you, absorbed into your being. Now you look from your own eyes with his vision.

The Temple of Aruhani

Walk now, with Aruhani's sight, to the Nayati of Julangis, Aruhani's temple. Take in details of the path and the approach to the Nayati. You will see the symbol of Julangis.

This is both the symbol of the Nayati and of the flow of its etheric energy. It can be used to augment magical workings with the energy of Aruhani's attributes. It may also be used as a symbol of healing to revitalise those who are weakened and withdrawn, and to reignite stagnant creativity. As a symbol of destruction it can be employed to dispel negative influences.

Enter Julangis and explore its chambers. Find a place that feels right to you and here sit down. Focus upon the symbol of Julangis and absorb it into yourself. Observe your own power to create and destroy and the wisdom needed to employ these forces wisely. Accept your own capacity to desire and create, whether artistically or through the conception of new life. Aruhani is the spark behind every creative thought, which you need before you can pull your creativity through into reality.

Conclusion of the Majhahn

When you are ready to conclude the majhahn, and return to the aganymphna flower. Here, sit down again, and allow your generated body to dissolve. Breathe in the body of light and allow it to energise you. Become conscious gradually of your physical body in your earthly Nayati and end the majhahn in your usual manner.

MAIRH VAIYAIRH

THE GOLDEN EYED

Guides and Companions

The rehuna will be familiar with creating dehara demitto from their Kaimana training, and within the Valley of Flowers that is Algoma it is also appropriate to fashion guides and companions who may be called upon for aid.

Sometimes, such dehara are created spontaneously within particular majhahns, and should this occur, it is often useful to continue working with these entities, to enrich the mutual relationship. These dehara might be symbolic of aspects of the rehuna's personality or of events in their lives. Interaction with such beings often reveals their true meaning.

Below are two examples of dehara demitto encountered by rehunas during their work on Algoma.

Mair Vayairh the Golden-Eyed

He is tall, quite angular, dressed in brown hooded robes, with the fabric having a subtle golden sheen. When the hood is cast back, his hair is braided and pinned up on his head in quite a complicated style, while other thin braids hang down his back and over his shoulders. There are long decorative pins through the top-knots of braids – dark gold in colour.

His skin is dark brown, but veined with golden glowing lines like intricate tattoos. The lines are thin, and pulse with this golden light. His eyes are orbs of intense smoking gold, but sometimes 'condense' into fully orange-gold eyes with cat's eye pupils. He also shows fangs when he smiles, but not in the manner of a vampire. More like a cat.

His hands are long-fingered and expressive, with cat's claws.

When I first encountered Mair Vayairh he told me he 'came from another realm' but that he was present to accompany me through Algoma and beyond. He spoke of himself as both 'the light and the shadow' in that he encompassed both within one form.

His appearance reminded me strongly of Aruhani's realm, which I always see as soaring dark peaks, gilded by a buttery light, and the sky is often rich gold, like a sunset over this dark land. Maybe, for me, he is an expression, or scion, of Aruhani.

He led me up the Stairs of Aloyt, and when we passed through the gate, I found myself in a visualised setting I've not visited for many years. This is an expression of eternal Spring, an orchard of blossoming fruit trees. The grass is lush underfoot and starred with white flowers. The air is full of drifting petals. The trees are immense, unlike natural fruit trees. Their main trunks are not particularly tall, but the foliage – or blossom – fills the landscape. Difficult to describe as it's somewhat dreamlike. You cannot see the sky. There is an overall an impression of immensity, almost brooding, as if a storm is massing beyond the tree canopies. But it is also very beautiful. This was a place I used to visit when resolving or investigating a particular magical situation. It can be no coincidence it presents itself again now.

Mair Vayairh showed me that Pyralis is done with, and can be formally acknowledged as complete. While this period of learning was not marked by an abundance of rituals, or formal magical acts, the lessons were mostly conducted in the physical world. Acceptance, assimilation, progress.

HARRAHN

Harrahn, Dehar of Restfulness

Harrahn is blue, and the mere touch of his cool hand is enough to banish all anxiety, terror, grief, distraction and misery from your heart. His eyes are pale lilac and he is dressed in gossamer veils.

I encountered him in a temple of classical design – pale marble columns, a high and airy chamber, with one wall open to the sky. There was a central pool, with a fountain, but the water trickled down subtly from its central statue of a har, rather than spurted and splashed. I saw that I was high up on a mountain and far below was the sparkling ocean. The very air in that temple seemed to breathe softly; a sense of drowsy content stole through me.

The dehar emerged from the shadows at the far end of the temple chamber, his veils floating around him. He exuded an ambience of absolute calm and bade me be seated before him. I saw then there were dark blue cushions on the floor for this purpose.

I told him I was seeking serenity and had simply found myself in this place.

He said to me that he cannot cure ills, but his temple is a haven of respite where you can recover your strengths temporarily. He warned that to try and dwell forever in his abode would be to abandon life. He is a dehar of forgetfulness. He said you should not drink of the waters in his temple, unless you wish to seek oblivion.

The Hienamas of the Tribes

Wraeththu: born in hate and bitterness, flexing their young, animal-strong muscles in the cities of the north. Always learning, always increasing their craft and cunning. Increasing. It was inevitable that eventually it touched somehar who had the curiosity, the intelligence to probe within the mystery. Wraeththu lost its ungoverned, adolescent wildness: It became an occult society, hungry for knowledge. But what they found within the Temple appalled them, its vastness scared them. Some broke away from the search for truth and fell back into the old ways of fighting and living for the day. Those who remained faced the unavoidable truth: Humanity was on the wane, Wraeththu waxed to replace it.

Wraeththu grouped into tribes, each ascribing to varying beliefs, but all united in the Wraeththu spirit.

From 'The Enchantments of Flesh and Spirit'

The tribes of Wraeththu each have an egregore, a personality based on the collective will and intention of the tribe members. The hienamas of each tribe have particular traits and strengths that rehunas and hienamas might draw upon. As part of Algoma training, an aspirant hienama should explore the beliefs and customs of the tribes, speaking with their hienamas in visualisation in order to explore their experiences and the development of harish spirituality.

Primordial Tribes

There are many different tribes, all of them with their own personality, customs and quirks. The initial tribes, primarily found in the continent of Megalithica, are known as the primordial tribes. From these many other tribes developed as hara broke away from the larger groups to pursue their own visions and ambitions.

Becoming acquainted with the primordial tribes, specifically their hienamas, gives insight into how the Deharan system of magic developed, from its roots to its flowering.

After performing majhahns to these hienamas, the rehuna may, if they wish, visit the hienamas of other tribes, and a selection of some of them is given in the appendices of this grimoire.

Uigenna

Infamous for their savagery, the Uigenna were the first organised tribe to appear in Megalithica. Most tribes on this continent can trace their lineage back to this group – with the occasional exception. They lacked organisation, and entered into a doomed association with the Varrs, which eventually led to their downfall. Many hara who were incepted into the Uigenna eventually broke away to join other, more organised and less brutal tribes, or else left to form their own tribes.

The Uigenna were an ungoverned maelstrom of base instincts, drawn together through the simple need to survive. As humans were incepted to Wraeththu, many brutally and against their will, so the fear, confusion and resentment they felt were expressed in their behaviour. The Uigenna were like feral infants, wild and directionless, lacking knowledge or experience, with no adults to guide them.

The hienama of the Uigenna, if he can be called that, is the Inceptor. He desires to make change, and the only way he can do that is by creating new hara. He doesn't yet have the knowledge or experience to use his abilities properly. He has powers, but uses them without thinking.

In terms of caste ascension, this hienama represents a basic interest in magic. The rehuna should visualise meeting him in the ruins of a ravaged city, where the first feral tribes grew strong. How does this har justify his actions? How does he view the powers he senses but does not fully understand? It's likely he'll become defensive if challenged or questioned too pointedly. He is like a surly teenager who thinks they know everything, when in fact they know very little.

Unneah

The Unneah are an offshoot of the Uigenna, comprised of hara who shunned the aggressive ways of the parent tribe, and who wished to create a more harmonious way of living, focusing on learning about their new state of being and becoming proficient in their blossoming abilities. They were the first to search for spiritual knowledge and from that developed the caste ascension system now practiced by almost all hara. The Unneah were one of the earliest tribes of Megalithica. They were the initial builders, the first to start imposing order upon chaos.

The hienama of the Unneah can be seen as one of the first hara to explore deeply the spiritual side of harish nature, and to experiment with harish abilities. He is concerned mainly with self-realisation, with 'waking up', and is himself a novice, poised at the brink of vast discoveries. The rehuna should meet him in visualisation in a fairly undeveloped settlement – a small human village or town that has been appropriated by the tribe, or else in a camp, since some early Unneah phyles were nomadic. The Unneah were influenced greatly by shamanic traditions of earlier times.

Varr

The Varrs were the first properly organised tribe in Megalithica. While as ferocious as the Uigenna in some respects, they were more disciplined and sophisticated than earlier hara. The tribe was formed by two Uigenna defectors, Ponclast and Terzian, who scorned the Uigenna for their crude society. They were the first to establish some kind of civilisation, but were hampered by Ponclast's (in particular) warped view of his harish condition. He saw Wraeththu's androgynous form as a debased mutation, a curse rather than a gift, and sought to recreate two genders within his hara and thus symbolises a fear of evolution and change. His apparent hatred of his own kind, as well as of humanity, led to cruel excesses. Eventually, other, smaller tribes rallied to end Ponclast's hold over Megalithica and called upon the ever-strengthening Gelaming for aid.

Once the Gelaming routed Ponclast in his fortress of Fulminir, the Varrs were rendered 'extinct'. The remains of the tribe – the ordinary hara who were farmers and traders – became the tribe of Parasiel. Those who refused to acknowledge alliance with the Gelaming fled or were taken captive.

A rehuna visiting this hienama should imagine going back in time, to before the Varrs were vanquished. The hienama will appear as either strongly soume or strongly ouana in aspect. He advocates a scientific approach to exploring psychic abilities and the effects of the mind upon the physical world. He has no time for mysticism and while inquisitive can be rigid in his thinking. He has a disciplined approach to his development and advocates self-discipline. To him, psychic abilities are as physical as hearing and sight. The rehuna could meet with this hienama in a Varrish location they deem most suitable, whether that's the black fortress of Fulminir or else the farming settlement of Galhea – these locations reflect two aspects of the Varrs.

Sulh

After leaving Megalithica, following the creation of the Wraeththu race, Thiede travelled east, pausing on his way in the island kingdom of Alba Sulh. Here, he incepted hara who would eventually become the tribe of Sulh. Influenced by the ancient, misty and eerie landscape in which they were created, the Sulh are a mystical, magical and erudite tribe, well-respected among Wraeththukind. They are often found as advisors to phyle leaders, in many parts of the world. Most Sulh adhere to a Pagan system of magic, aligned to nature and the seasons, but within the leadership cabals of high-ranking hara favour a more ceremonial and formal approach to magic, involving complex rituals. The Sulh, while spiritually mature, are rather a proud tribe, who tend to patronise those they consider to be less developed than themselves.

The Hienama of the Sulh is a teacher, gentle in most respects, although somewhat exacting in others. His negative trait is that he represents the pride that may develop in a student rehuna, leading to egotism and delusions of grandeur. More positively, he expects a rehuna to work on themselves rigorously, to study without distraction. He grants increased self-awareness, and makes use of scrying and 'mirrors' such as sacred pools. This hienama should be met in a natural location of Alba Sulh – by a sacred lake, within a mysterious forest, or amid misty mountains.

Kakkahaar

The Kakkahaar were founded by Velisarius, one of the most influential of Uigenna defectors, who before his inception had already undergone medical training. What he learned during his human education he carried with him into his Wraeththu life. He was convinced hara should study and understand their new condition, and probe the boundaries of their capabilities. Like Orien, the founder of the Sarocks, he took his followers into seclusion within a desert, but further south than Saltrock.

Velisarius' ideals eventually took the Kakkahaar down strange and questionable avenues, especially once he withdrew from public life and handed the reins of the fledgling tribe to his protégé, Lianvis. Over time, as Lianvis matured and entered into alliances with other tribes, the Kakkahaar's magical practices softened somewhat – a condition demanded by the Gelaming – but while they might have adopted a more benign façade, if only superficially, they are still treated with caution. Part of their mystique is that they won't flinch from taking the harshest action, should they feel it is merited. The tribe is nomadic and deft in the darker regions of magic. They are powerful and often feared, although their aid is sought in times of dire need.

The hienama of the Kakkahaar is impatient with rehunas held back by fear and who wince from the dark corners they come across in their training. He represents caution thrown to the winds – a reckless approach to magic. He believes that any means justifies a desired end and magical training to him is no different from an inception: if it works, good, if not, and a rehuna is damaged or driven mad, they must have been weak and are no loss. There is also within him the possibility that power corrupts. The positive qualities in this hienama are courage, self-belief, self-confidence and determination. He is honest and lacks any form of false sentimentality. He is best visited in the ancient ruins favoured by the Kakkahaar for their rituals, deep beneath the desert sands.

Colurastes

Known as the Serpent Hara, the Colurastes are among the most enigmatic of tribes. The serpent has long been a symbol of wisdom within magic, and also has the reputation of being the great seducer. The Colurastes have a great affinity with serpents, and have mutated somewhat to be like them. Their hair is alive and can be used like limbs. They can be unpredictable and dangerous, hired often as assassins and spies, occupations for which they have a natural propensity. However, they are also very skilled in herbal lore and healing. They were, in their early days, renowned for having the best success rate with inceptions. They make their communities in caves, preferring to live underground.

The founder of the Colurastes was Sciamander, who was almost certainly originally a Kakkahaar. There are many legends concerning how he changed and formed his tribe, became serpent-like in some respects. But nohar really knows the truth.

The rehuna wishing to meet with the hienama of the Colurastes will have to first win him over and gain his trust. Colurastes are suspicious of outsiders and reluctant to share their knowledge. Therefore, a rehuna should take offerings to him, and be prepared to fulfil a task or take on a challenge. He represents the most mystical aspect of magic, that which might draw many to it in the first place. He is alluring and promises the revelation of great secrets. His negative trait is insularity and the risk of becoming too inward-looking. The ideal location to meet with this hienama is in a secluded chamber of a vast cave complex in which his tribe resides. The chamber will be his Nayati.

Sarock

The Sarock are a small but important tribe, based in the desert town Saltrock, in southwest Megalithica, situated close to a vast soda lake. They are industrious, peaceful and known for their honesty. The Sarock are builders and pioneers, and in their early days were employed by Thiede, the first Wraeththu, to find and recruit the best inceptees for him. These carefully-selected new hara formed the tribe of Gelaming, Thiede's own tribe, deriving from all human races, and all corners of the world.

The Sarock were initially formed by Orien, the first human incepted by Thiede, and therefore the second Wraeththu to be created. His aim was to create a perfect, self-sufficient community, and to achieve this he left the Uigenna early on. Orien was appalled at the direction many hara he had incepted had taken, and felt he needed distance from the barbarity of the crumbling cities in order to create a harmonious society, in which hara could reach for their true potential. The harsh conditions of the desert and the soda lake meant the Sarocks enjoyed their seclusion for a long time. In essence, they were a 'hidden' tribe until Pellaz Har Aralis came to power as Tigron in Immanion.

The hienama with whom the rehuna meets in visualisation can only be Orien, this wise and gentle and soul, the first hienama of all, the first harish spiritual teacher. He is associated with individuation, pioneering, self-sufficiency and self-reliance. He teaches a rehuna how to listen to their 'inner voice', the core of wisdom within. He is also concerned with a rehuna's destiny. He should be met in the town of Saltrock, a fairly large settlement of wooden buildings, hidden deep within the southern desert.

Gelaming

Created by Thiede, the founder of Wraeththu, the Gelaming comprise the most advanced of hara, and were recruited from tribes around the world. They possess the ancestral knowledge of all human races and are for the most part enlightened and erudite. The beauty of their capital, Immanion, is legendary. Gelaming have mastered superior magic that allows them feats impossible for other tribes.

The Gelaming can be represented by the Emperor card in the Tarot. They have the potential for wisdom, but this can become twisted into a passive-aggressive form of tyranny. They can be seen as Uigenna evolved, but as they are made up predominantly of hara from early tribes, (from all over the world), some of the early aspects lie deeply buried within them. The Gelaming's worst trait is the belief they know what's right for everyhar and that other tribes should defer to their superior knowledge.

The hienama of this tribe would be aware of its negative traits; he is a highly-trained and experienced har after all. He has vast knowledge and much to teach, but he might have a rather inflated opinion of himself. So while the rehuna can learn from this hienama they should bear in mind he is in some ways restricted by his own beliefs. The positive aspect of this hienama is his open mind to all forms of magic. He has a strong sense of tolerance and compassion, and the wisdom to know what action to take in any situation. He is never driven by greed, fear or spite. The rehuna may meet him in any location in or around Immanion – the pale, lovely city itself with its serene nayatis, or on the forest clad hills behind the city where ancient shrines may be found.

Divozenky - Mind of the Earth

He sensed a mighty presence become aware of him. It was almost impossible to describe, but he felt it throughout his being and beyond. He sank back into a vast sentience that had been with him all along, yet he'd been unaware of it. Sometimes he'd glimpsed it in the ecstasies of aruna, felt it stirring his soul in the forest around Samway, tasted it in spring air, but this was far more intense. He was filled with an immense feeling that was part joy, part awe, part fear. He was sinking into the earth itself, falling back, supported and known.

And the earth spoke to him. This was not in words, but in impressions. This was the moment when the tiny parasite becomes aware of the creature upon and from which it lives. It realises that the sweet blood it sups is alive, and part of something greater.

From *'The Ghosts of Blood and Innocence'*

Within the Deharan system, worlds are regarded as sentient beings, benevolent and tolerant hosts of the emerging species that grow upon them, such as humanity and hara. Wraeththu have an instinctive imperative to nurture a better relationship with their home planet than humanity did, to take seriously their responsibility as caretakers of the earth and its creatures. Part of Algoma training involves a rehuna forging their own relationship with the mind of the world. Algoma in essence is experiencing the natural world fully, after the hardships of Acantha and Pyralis. What began in Kaimana, with the investigation of the seasonal wheel of the year and its festivals, is now taken further.

The earth is known within Deharan magic as Divozenky, a name coined by the tribe of Nezreka in Anakhai, an area corresponding roughly to the Czech Republic of the human world. The myths surrounding Divozenky include tales of her guardians, the Krim Sri, who are said to dwell in an underground city that allows access to the mind of the world. The Krim Sri are a race that predate humanity and live in concealment. In Wraeththu lore, it's believed humanity derived from the Krim Sri in ancient times, but whatever the initial relationship might have been, the Krim Sri had no desire to communicate with what humanity became. However, they have lowered the barriers somewhat with hara. The legends state that when the Krim Sri first came out of the ethers to earth, they too were androgynous beings, but mutated into separate genders in order to conceal themselves among the creatures of the their new world. Regarded as nature spirits in their own land, the Krim Sri are in fact the remains of a once-powerful nation.

All encounters with Divozenky take place traditionally with the help of the Krim Sri. Therefore, the visualised journey into the mind of the world begins with a visit to Helek Sah, the city of the Krim Sri. This partly mirrors the underworld journey of the descent into Xephelax, in that seven gateways have to be passed. But the purpose this time is to access Divozenky, and the visualised etheric realm where rehunas can speak with her. (Divozenky is referred to by the feminine pronoun, but is in fact beyond gender. The feminine here reflects the concept she has often been regarded as a mother goddess, throughout human history.)

A Visit to Helek Sah and the Mind of Divozenky

Construct your etheric Nayati in the usual manner and compose yourself within it. Summon a portal that will lead to Anakhai, and the entrance to the realm of the Krim Sri.

Step through the portal and find yourself standing before a soaring cliff face covered in hanging ivy. Pull aside a part of the drape, so that you can place your hands against the stone. Say: 'I call upon the Krim Sri to grant me access to Helek Sah and to guide me to the realm of Divozenky that I might speak with her. In the name of the Aghama, give me entrance.'

The fabric of the stone begins to alter – not by glowing or becoming transparent, but by its very atoms being agitated. The rock shivers. You hear a murmuring voice say: 'Then have faith and walk through the stone.'

Take a deep breath and step forward. The matrix of the stone has become somehow loose and you are able to pass through it, while at the same time knowing it is still solid. You feel a faint pressure against your skin and a squeezing sensation in your head.

Eventually, you emerge into a narrow, spiralling passageway with a low ceiling. You have to stoop to walk along it. The path gradually descends and grows narrower, and the ceiling becomes lower, the air almost unbreathable. You are bent nearly double and feel very uncomfortable, but you know that the discomforts of the journey are essential, an intrinsic part of what you're doing.

Just as you think you must pass out from lack of oxygen, the passageway disgorges you into a cavern. You take a gulp of air in relief and stand up straight to stretch your cramped limbs and back. The scene before you is lit by a single enormous torch that rests upon a black metal stand. The cave before you is full of water, with only a narrow beach. Silvery grey damp sand shifts beneath your feet. The beach extends only a short way; beyond it black water stretches out into a void that seems endless to your eyes. You can't see the farther shore, or even perceive if there is one. The air is humid. Your breath steams, yet you don't feel cold.

A dark shape glides across the dark waters – a long narrow boat. At prow and stern are carvings of what look like a strange hybrid of eagle, horse and fish. The pilot is a tall thin figure robed in black, reminding you of the archetypal underworld boatman. He stands at the stern, using a single large oar to propel the boat forward. Eventually, the boat comes to rest near the water's edge.

Climb into the boat, after which the pilot silently turns the vessel and it slides smoothly into the darkness. You're aware of immense space around you, even though you can't see it. A single lantern at the prow casts a small pool of radiance over the water.

You reach the far shore and disembark. The boat once again drifts off into darkness and you survey your surroundings. A corridor of torches on tall metal stands line a sandy path that leads to a rock face. The flames of the torches are blue. At the end of the path, covering an arched entrance in the rock, is a wall of roaring red flames. You know this is the Gate of Flame, the first portal you must pass through to reach Helek Sah.

Say: 'I call upon the Krim Sri to grant me entrance through the ward of flame. Guide me through the gates and into the realm of Divozenky so I might speak with her.'

The wall of flames draws back like curtains, and a tall, thin figure walks beneath the stone arch revealed before you. This appears to be a woman, clad in a dark robe with a high collar that rises behind her neck in a stiff fan. Her hair is confined in

181

a strange and complicated metal headdress, a mass of spikes and waving tines. Her neck is swathed in close-fitting necklaces of dark jewels, so that no patch of skin can be seen. She carries a black staff tipped with a golden ornament of a bird of prey.

The figure bows and says, 'I am Tiy, Eye Priestess of the Krim Sri. You are welcome in Helek Sah. Follow me.'

Go with her into a deep gorge beyond the portal. The rock is bare and occasionally running with damp. The air smells of earth. Looking up, you can see only darkness. Torches that line the walls are dim.

Tiy does not speak but leads the way quickly. Soon, you reach a second gate, which is a violent cataract of water across the path. 'The Gate of Water,' Tiy says. She raises her arms and draws symbols in the air with her staff. Finally, she utters a tone, and the water draws back like the fire at the first portal did, as if it is merely curtains of fabric. Pass through and walk on.

The third gate across the gorge is of stone, covered in carvings of tall winged figures. 'The Gate of Earth,' Tiy says. She opens it simply by knocking upon it with her staff. Beyond this gate a perilous walkway of stone arcs across a deep chasm.

On the far side of this rock bridge, you enter another chasm lit by flickering torchlight. Here, after a hundred yards or so, you come to a gate constructed entirely of dark metal. 'The Gate of Iron,' Tiy says. Again she employs her staff to open it.

Tiy leads you onwards until you come to a place where the path seems blocked by what you can only sense as 'nothingness'. You peer into endless darkness.

'This is the Gate of Trackless Void,' Tiy says. 'It is part in this world, part in the otherlanes.' She raises her arms before the gate and murmurs a few words in a language you don't recognise. She then hums some musical tones. After this, she beckons to you and says: 'Come, it is open.'

You step into the void. It feels as if you are crossing the universe with a single step. It generates a strange feeling of euphoria, as if a secret of life has been revealed. You are inside the gate for only a couple of seconds, yet time stretches to eternity. When you step onto the firm path beyond, it feels as if you've woken from a long sleep.

Again, Tiy beckons for you to follow and the path turns a corner to the right, revealing the sixth gate. It appears as whirling nebulae of sparkling light. 'This is the Gate of Stars,' Tiy says. As before, she utters sounds to open the gate. When you step through it, you feel as if your entire being is filled with light. It is like becoming a star. On the other side, you feel refreshed, full of energy.

The last obstacle is the Gate of Bones. It's a reminder you are in the earthly realm, after the heady experiences of the previous two gates, since this final portal is made entirely of bones. To open it, Tiy simply pulls a key from a pocket of her robe and unlocks it.

Beyond the final gate, the path becomes much wider. The rock walls to either side are smooth and set with globes of soft yellow radiance.

The path turns another corner to reveal an immense cave, the city of Helek Sah. It is a city of many levels, lit by flame. The architecture is unlike anything you've seen before – immense buildings of strange design. Tiy leads the way through a maze of streets. You see a few Krim Sri going about their daily business, pausing only to bow their heads to Tiy as she walks among them. Both males and females could be mistaken for hara, since they are androgynous in appearance.

The buildings are tall and narrow, comprised of obsidian. The pavement beneath your feet is like black glass, yet not slippery. Tiy leads you to a dark tower, which you enter and climb. At the top you emerge into a chamber, which is empty of furniture. The floorboards are painted with a large circle of symbols; a place to work magic.

Tiy gestures for you to be seated within the circle. You know this is her workroom, and also the place where she guides visitors to Divozenky. There are no tools here, for the only tool she uses is her mind.

Once you're seated, Tiy sits down cross-legged before you and reaches out to put her hands upon your shoulders. At her request, you close your eyes. You have a sense of the room growing immense around you. It's as if you're sitting in a vast cavern, and the walls are breathing.

Tiy's voice begins to vibrate low tones. These sounds weave in the air like twin serpents of vapour. They wind around each other, forming a double helix, until it is one serpent eating its own tail. This is a representation of the building block of life. The serpent is all around you. You are part of it, as is everything else upon the earth. The sounds weave visions in your head; the song of creation. You are melting into it, becoming sound yourself, a sigh upon the air.

Now you sense a mighty presence become aware of you. You sink back into a vast sentience that has been with you all your life. Sometimes you've felt it stirring your soul in a forest, or have tasted it in springtime air, but this is far more intense. You're filled with an immense feeling that is part joy, part awe, part fear. You're sinking into the earth itself, falling back, supported and known. And the earth speaks to you – not in words, but in impressions.

Open your eyes and find yourself standing upon a high hilltop beneath the light of the moon. A grove of trees surrounds the brow of the hill: birch and oak. You hear the song of night birds and the trill of crickets in the summer grasses. An endless landscape spreads out below, lush and untouched. A pale shape moves at the edge of your vision and you turn to see a woman walking towards you across the soft grass of the hill. She is barefoot, clad in close-fitting trousers and tunic that appeared to be made entirely of leaves and feathers. Her long hair is red, its colour visible even in the moonlight. Her eyes glow with blue and green light – the colours of both sea and sky. You know in your heart who she is, the heart of the world, the Rose. You've known her all your life: the spirit of the earth itself. And she knows you too – as she knows every soul that lives upon her skin.

She comes right up to you and links one of her arms through one of yours, indicating you should walk together. She feels as real to you as any person you know in reality. You can smell the perfume of her; cut grass, pine needles, rain, ripe fruit and summer flowers.

She tells you that you are in a realm within a realm. There are many other beings here, but at this moment you can't see them. All the gods and entities dreamed up by humans and hara throughout history reside in this place. The cities and landscapes of the world's mind are realised ideals – the mountains touch the heavens, the seas are vast beyond imagining, the forests never-ending and full of magic.

Walk now with Divozenky and explore the realm of her mind. Speak with her. She may have tasks for you. You may meet other entities in her realm.

When you are ready to conclude the meditation, create a portal for yourself back into your etheric Nayati. Thank Divozenky for her presence and then go through the portal. Conclude the majhahn in the usual way.

After performing this meditation, you should at the earliest opportunity find a spot within the landscape where you can commune with Divozenky in reality. Leave an offering for her there, and vow to work to respect her body, helping to protect and nurture her in whatever small ways you can.

CONSTELLATUS

ASTRACLAUSTRI

Constellati: The Walkers Between the Stars

After the Divozenky majhahn, which confirms the rehuna's connection with their home world, they now reach out to commune with cosmic entities. This forms part of the preparation for the creation of a spiritual pearl, which is the Algoma ascension majhahn.

During Nahir Nuri training, the rehuna will venture beyond earthly boundaries and focus upon the realms within the ethers and the otherlanes. This will also involve creating realms in which to undergo the training for each tier of Nahir Nuri. As part of the conclusion of Algoma, the rehuna begins preparation for this later work. They will commune with Astraclaustri, a Constellatus and the gatekeeper of the cosmos.

The Constellati are beings of the ethers and the otherlanes that represent the stars and the myriad formations among them. They are avatars of the intelligence of the universe. The body of a Constellatus is composed entirely of motes of light that appear to us like stars. These immense beings are also known as Star Walkers, or the Walkers Between the Stars. They have a protective role, in that they are caretakers of the cosmos, but they are also repositories of knowledge. Within their substance they record all the pathways of the universe, and the myriad worlds. The rehuna may call upon these entities as guides, as teachers, even as vehicles. They may ask them to open up portals into the otherlanes, the hidden ways between the stars and the realms of existence. But the Constellati will only commune fully with beings of certain level of knowledge and experience. The ascension to Algoma, and subsequent Nahir Nuri training, (should the rehuna wish to take their studies that far), gives access to these beings. For the rehuna approaching Algoma, it's appropriate only to approach Astraclaustri the gatekeeper.

Astraclaustri: Gatekeeper of the Cosmos

Construct your etheric Nayati in the usual manner.

Visualise a portal opening before you, beyond which at first you can see only darkness. But when you pass through this portal, you find yourself upon a transparent platform that hangs among the stars. All around you are nebulae, galaxies and constellations, exploding with life and events. You see huge cosmic clouds and strange pulses of light. The sky from Earth seems empty in comparison, for here there seems no darkness at all, simply incomprehensibly huge blasts of light and energy.

You sense the countless worlds and stars of the universe, and beyond that, the layers of reality that comprise the multiverse. You feel as if you are standing upon a threshold and know that unimaginable journeys are to come, but for now you are here to prepare for your Algoma ascension, the creation of a spiritual pearl.

Call upon Astraclaustri: 'Astale, Astraclaustri, Star Walker, Gatekeeper of the Cosmos. I ask you to manifest before me, to show me a glimpse of the wonders you contain. Prepare my body for Algoma ascension, imbue my being with stellar energy to empower the spiritual pearl I will create.'

As you gaze upon the stars, you perceive movement within this dizzying vista. A being of light, of unimaginable proportions, appears to be forming from the stars themselves.

This is Astraclaustri. As he draws closer to you, his form becomes smaller, so that he may commune with you easily, but even so, he is a towering creature, his hands the size of houses. He holds out a hand to you, and you know you may step onto it. Astraclaustri lifts you gently and puts you upon his shoulder.

He does not speak but you perceive his words in your mind. He reveals to you the snaking pathways of the otherlanes, the nodes of light that represent portals to other realms. He tells you this will be your place of work in the future, that you will create realms for yourself, not just a Nayati but – if you so desire it – a whole world dedicated to your studies, a vast library, workplace, laboratory and theatre.

He tells you to concentrate carefully and to perceive the astral mites that skitter around you. These are tiny, almost invisible creatures of light. Astraclaustri tells you to call one of these mites to you, to take it into your being, so that you may infuse the pearl you will make with its energy. Through this, the fruit of the pearl will be part cosmic, part earthly.

When this is done, you know it is time to depart, but you will return in the future. Thank Astraclaustri for his assistance, and then ask him to return you to the platform upon which you first arrived. From there, return through the portal to your etheric Nayati.

Sit for some moments within your Nayati, aware of the warmth of the astral mite within you. It will lie dormant, waiting for the spiritual pearl to be created.

When you are ready, conclude the majhahn in your usual manner.

The Spiritual Pearl

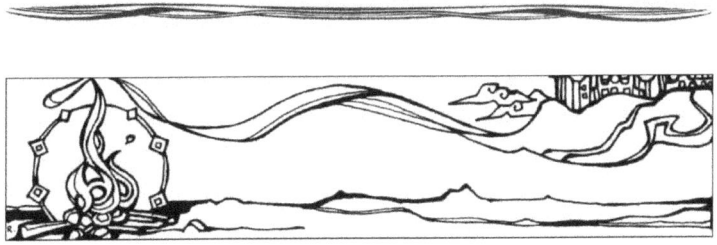

Algoma Ascension Majhahn

In order to experience caste ascension to the rank of Algomalid hienama, the rehuna must first recreate themselves within a spiritual pearl. To initiate this procedure, the rehuna creates the pearl through breathing techniques.

Prior to embarking upon the work, the rehuna should choose a patron dehar to work with them during this phase, who is not one of the Dehara Vegrandis (since they have a separate role to play). This should be a dehar with whom the rehuna feels a particular rapport, and who 'feels' appropriate for this part of caste ascension. The rehuna may, if they so choose, create a dehar specifically for this purpose.

The creation of the spiritual pearl can't be accomplished within one majhahn, but requires at least a fortnight of preliminary work.

For all majhahns of this process, the rehuna should prepare themselves, both in reality and within their etheric Nayati, as they did for their previous ascensions. The first step is Pearl Breathing, which generates the nascent pearl.

Pearl Breathing

Sit within your etheric Nayati and compose yourself for meditation.

Touching the tongue to the roof of the mouth, breathe in through the nose for a count of five, simultaneously contracting your stomach muscles, thereby pulling the belly inwards. Hold for a count of five, and then release the breath through the mouth for a count of five, this time pushing your belly outwards.

Continue this breathing method for a few minutes, all the time focusing your attention upon the area within your body that corresponds to the Cauldron of Creation – roughly where the second sikra lies. Visualise that this area gradually fills with, and becomes empowered by, agmara energy that pulsates in time to your breathing.

After a further few minutes of this focused, rhythmic breathing, direct your attention to the base sikra and the genital area. Direct the agmara, with each breath you inhale, into the genitals, while on exhaling, take the agmara back up into the cauldron of creation.

When you feel comfortable with this part of the procedure, take it further.

On each inhalation, direct agmara down from the Cauldron of Creation into the genitals, and from there up the spine to around the area when the third sikra resides. On each exhalation, direct the agmara back down into the Cauldron of Creation.

Once you feel comfortable with this part of the cycle, extend the breathing.

Now, on each inhalation, direct agmara down from the Cauldron of Creation to the genitals, and from there up the central axis of the body to the crown of the head, just below where the seventh sikra lies. Then, on exhaling, direct the agmara back down into the Cauldron of Creation.

Continue this cycle of breathing for a further few minutes.

Now, call upon your patron dehar.

Visualise the dehar sitting closely before you and join hands with him. When you inhale, the dehar exhales. Take his breath into you, incorporating it into your cycle of breathing, so that the dehar's breath and energy vitalises your own.

When you exhale, the dehar takes your breath into himself and empowers it.

This circulation of agmara gradually forms the pearl within the Cauldron of Creation. See this as a softly-glowing sphere. This pearl should not be visualised as containing a new har, but as a vessel for your own spiritual essence, being prepared for caste ascension. At this point, do not attempt to place your essence into the growing pearl.

This exercise should be performed daily for at least two weeks prior to the majhahn of caste ascension.

Moving Essence into the Spiritual Pearl

After the period of creating the spiritual pearl, you should now perform a majhahn to project your essence into it.

Create your Nayati in the usual manner and invoke your patron dehar, with whom you have been working on creating the spiritual pearl.

Again, build up a cycle of energy exchange between you, so that you are gently breathing together.

Visualise that you are sitting opposite your patron dehar but with a space of a couple of feet between you. The dehar holds out his arms, the hands directed towards you. Visualise that the pearl within you glows with a soft radiance and pulses like a heart.

The dehar draws symbols upon the air and murmurs a ritual chant. Visualise that your essence, the part of you that will be raised to Algoma, is drawn by the dehar to enter the pearl, where it will mature and be nourished for three days.

During this time, you are the zero, the unborn, for three whole days.

Empowerment of Earth and Stars

Before you perform the majhahn that births the pearl, first imbue it with the energy of earth and stars, which you gained from your visit to Divozenky and Astraclaustri.

Sit within your Nayati and, holding your hands over your belly, visualise the spirit of Divozenky entering the pearl, nourishing and strengthening it, endowing creativity and compassion.

Then, when this is done, wake the astral mite that has been waiting within you. See it as a pinprick of stellar lustre that enters into the pearl, endowing knowledge, courage and inventiveness.

See these essences mingling, coagulating, finalising the creation of the pearl. When this is done, the essence within is ready to emerge.

The Majhahn of Emergence

Unlike a pearl born to a har, the spiritual pearl does not take weeks to mature. On the day of the Majhahn of Emergence pay special attention to the preparation of yourself and your Nayati. Take a ritual bath, and decorate your earthly Nayati with season foliage and flowers. Music and incense should also be appropriate for the majhahn to come.

Once you have constructed your Nayati on both an earthly and etheric level, sit within it and paint the symbols of the major dehara upon your body, along with any sigils or symbols that have personal significance for you.

Call upon your patron dehar to be present, as well as the four major dehara and the Aghama.

While these dehara stand around you, encourage the pearl to be born, to pass from you into reality. You may visualise this as the pearl emanating from the cauldron of creation through your skin, or you may visualise it emerging as a normal pearl would do, through the soume-lam.

Once it is before you, take it in your hands. You perceive

movement within it. As you watch, the surface of the pearl becomes transparent and begins to break. A being of light emerges from it and this you take into yourself. The light fills your being: this is both your rebirth and your ascension.

Feel the energy of this essence, comprised of your own will and intention, the dehara, the cosmos and the earth, flowing through you. You feel as immense as a Constellatus, radiating stellar light. You are aware of the presence of Divozenky, giving this process her blessing. Bask in these feelings and impressions for as long as you wish.

Your patron dehar will formally conclude the ascension with a short ceremony to attune you to the symbol Algoma, which he transfers to you through his gaze, his breath, his hands, or through aruna.

After this, he pronounces you Algomalid, a hienama in your own right.

Thiede's Domain

It is a hidden palace, at the end of a lonely back road of the otherlanes.

From 'The Shades of Time and Memory'

The culmination of Ulani involves a visit to Thiede, avatar of The Aghama, in the hidden realm he designed to be a private temple where initiates only of Algoma level or higher might commune with him.

By this point, the rehuna has ventured through experiences both dark and light to reach the threshold of Nahir Nuri, the caste of endless learning, and the realisation that to learn is better than to know.

Thiede, who suffered his own trials, his own rise and fall through hubris, and a subsequent redemption through overcoming his weaknesses, can be regarded as a spiritual mirror.

The Working

Enter your etheric Nayati and compose yourself for majhahn in your usual manner. Perform your preferred breathing exercises to enter into a meditative state. Visualise the etheric environment, the details of your Nayati that you created and expanded   upon

THIEDE

during your Ulani training. Examine the symbols and think of what they mean to you, what lessons they represent.

Now imagine that your surroundings are gradually fading away, as if eclipsed by a creeping darkness. Your senses become sluggish, almost as if you have been drugged. Gradually, you slip into a strange dreamless sleep.

Suddenly, you find yourself awake and in a completely new place. You can't yet see anything, but are aware of space around you; the echo of your breathing seems to indicate this. You must be in a vast room.

You perceive a pinprick of light in the darkness. It zooms towards you, growing in size, until it bobs in front of you, a sphere of radiance the size of your head. The sphere pulses a little, as if it were breathing.

This is the essence of The Aghama, the creative force of all things. You say to it: 'I have fought through the thorns. I have walked through the fire to the world below. I have crossed the valley of flowers. I have birthed the spiritual pearl. I am here, Thiede, before you.'

At these words, the sphere contracts until it's merely a blazing mote of brilliance, then it explodes with a dazzling display of sparks. You shield your eyes for a moment, afraid that the sizzling particles will burn your face. You can smell something like gunpowder, but you aren't burned. Light fills your environment.

You are in an almost unimaginably huge chamber, like a temple, its domed roof veined with organic struts and beams. There is a floor of polished obsidian. Standing upon it in rows are bowls of radiance on tripods seven feet tall. Beyond them, ranks of tall pillars disappear into the distance, like the reflections in multiple mirrors.

Before you, a tall figure manifests. He has long blood-red hair and eyes that can see through all. 'I am Thiede,' he says to you. 'You are welcome here. Follow me.'

You now follow Thiede through the apartments of his haven. Certain parts of it are alien to behold, while others appear similar to structures found on earth – temples, libraries, cathedrals.

Thiede brings you to a room that is spherical and made of black glass. This chamber begins to descend, shrinking as it does so to become a mere vessel. A light appears in the wall, which expands until it looks like a ring of flame. Through it, you can see the world outside. Thiede gestures for you to follow him through the portal.

The realm beyond appears to be an ancient world. The light is dim and a huge, red sun hangs in the sky, surrounded by a nimbus of purple flame. The landscape is flat, an endless vista of shining lakes, surrounded by drooping trees that are not willows, but like them.

You glance behind yourself and glimpse an impossible structure rearing up, which taxes the mind because of its strangeness and complexity.

Thiede leads you to the shore of the nearest lake, and here there is a seat among the trees. You sit down beside him.

'Now, tell me of your travels,' he says.

Looking into his eyes, you recount through word and image and sensation the experiences of your Ulani training. Perhaps you relive some of them to share with Thiede.

The final part of this working is to spend time with Thiede, assimilating any knowledge or advice he gives you. Explore his personal realm, while being aware that in future you too will be create realms like this and discover many more built by others. Spend as much time in this place as you wish.

When you are ready, bid farewell to Thiede, thank him for this meeting and for any gifts he might have given you. Close the majhahn in your usual manner.

This concludes the caste training of the Ulani tier.

The Role of Hienama

Now that the rehuna's Algoma training is complete, they are empowered to act as a hienama. If they so wish, they can offer ascension training to others, who would prefer not to work alone and would like guidance. A hienama can perform caste ascensions up to their own level. Examples of ascension majhahns are given in the Appendices, but hienamas are encouraged also to create their own majhahns.

A hienama may also perform rites of passage – bondings, namings, memorials – for which they should create their personal majhahns.

Some hienamas might choose to train further in healing techniques, should they have a calling in that direction.

It's advised that a hienama should wait at least three months before embarking upon Nahir Nuri training. Algoma is connected deeply with the earth – with our realm – and should be experienced as that fully before the hienama moves on to work in the ethers. It's essential to be grounded beforehand.

Appendices

Appendix I:
The Wraeththu Mythos
By Storm Constantine

The Wraeththu

In the novels, Wraeththu are a race of androgynous or hermaphrodite beings, (that is both male and female in one body), who come to replace humanity. A Wraeththu individual is called a 'har', and the plural is 'hara'. They live in tribes and while some of them are nomadic, others occupy settlements, towns and cities. They are physically perfect beings, their bodies more efficient and resistant to disease than those of humans. They are more in tune with the environment, and are naturally adept at magical practices. Initially, hara were created from humans by a transformation process known as inception. Wraeththu blood has the capacity to mutate human DNA, so that a simple transfusion is all that's required to transform a human into a Wraeththu har. Eventually, in the stories, hara reproduce amongst themselves and as humanity dwindles there are fewer individuals to incept anyway. The gods with whom Wraeththu interact are created in their own image. Wraeththu gods are called dehara, (singular: dehar).

The concept of the hermaphrodite has always been important in magical philosophy. It represents the union of opposites, true harmony of being. The word derives from the names of two Greek deities: the god Hermes and the goddess Aphrodite. I think it is an elegant term, but because it has acquired negative, almost sideshow, connotations, through earlier generations' misunderstanding of, and insensitivity to, people born with dual or unspecific gender, the word hermaphrodite is no longer a polite term to use in 'real life'. Magically, however, I think it's important to reclaim it as the spiritual symbol it is.

We live in a dualistic universe of opposites: male and female, light and dark, hot and cold and, of course, good and evil. The hermaphrodite symbolises the integration of these opposites. It is representative of DNA itself: the double helix, the twin serpent of the Caduceus wand, the Ouroboros snake of alchemy that bites its own tail. It combines the strengths of traditional male and female aspects; the passive and the active, the intuitive and the physical. In the Dehara system, practitioners visualise themselves as being androgynous in nature and the gods with whom they interact are also androgynous. By adopting this form, they step beyond the mundane limitations of the physical body.

As to what a har looks like, it should be seen as the perfect union of both genders, almost ethereal in appearance. Wraeththu do not have breasts (as they do not feed their young like humans do) or wide womanly hips, but neither are they bulging with muscles or 'triangular shaped' like the ideal of a male body. They are strong and agile, lean and fit.

While I usually refer to hara by the pronoun 'he', some people prefer a gender neutral pronoun instead. The least awkward of these is the singular pronoun set of 'they, them, their': i.e. 'ey', 'em', 'eir', etc.

Aruna or Sex Magic

Aruna: the exchange of essences. For Wraeththu, reproduction is just one aspect of physical communion. Its prime function for us is higher spiritual development. The har learns to refine its energy beyond mere pleasure. The hermaphrodite has long been regarded as a perfect archetype in many magical and religious systems. Humans struggled to understand and then strive spiritually for a concept that in us has become flesh. In alchemy, the androgyne is the rebus, the union of the alchemical king and queen, the fruit of the sacred marriage. In eastern systems, the balance of male and female principles was a desired quality: the harmony of yin and yang. We are a physical expression of the double helix, the entwined serpents. The feminine principle within us is called soume, and its organ is soume-lam. Magically, its main properties are coolness, moistness and passivity. The male principle is ouana, and its organ is ouana-lim. Its main magical properties are heat, dryness and activity. The generative organs are a microcosmic reflection of the main energy centres of the body. The har discovers the myriad uses to which these energies can be put during their training.

Thiede-har-Gelaming
'The Enchantments of Flesh and Spirit'

Sex between Wraeththu is termed aruna and is considered a spiritual practice. It is not simply a means for reproduction, but can be a majhahn that affects reality. It plays a big part in the novels, so cannot be ignored in the Deharan magical system. Androgynous sex is not something you can do in reality, but if you feel comfortable with the idea, you can visualise this activity in meditation. If you already have a sexual partner with whom you practice magic, then obviously you can experiment with the concept, but it is not an obligatory part of the system.

This system does not revolve purely around sex magic, because there are many other ways of interacting with universal energy, the Source, God, or whatever you want to call it. Sex magic is something that individuals can explore in their own way, if they feel so inclined. That said, many people who have worked with this system have reported they've 'taken aruna' with entities they've met in their visualisations, and that often knowledge has been imparted this way. The important thing to remember is to do only that with which you are comfortable. If you simply visualise yourself as a beautiful har during meditations, that is more than enough.

However, for those who wish to know more about aruna, here are the details. A har is both male and female and has all the required organs for this function. They can take a dominant or passive role in aruna, and do not have to stick to the same role. When visualising a harish partner, you can imagine them as an idealised version of yourself, the components of your male and female sides, your animus and anima. Aruna is not just about physical gratification. It is a spiritual practice, and a way to connect with the Source.

When Wraeththu reproduce, they create pearls, which are like eggs. The pearl is dropped by the hostling and then hatches a couple of weeks later. This concept is incorporated into the seasonal festivals, known as arojhahns, which is part of the Neoma level.

Inception

Hara become Aralids, (studying the first tier of the system), once they are incepted, i.e. once their human form is transformed. The ceremony in which this takes place is called Harhune. The early level of Dehara incorporates a Harhune visualisation, during which the practitioner creates for themselves an androgynous form for Dehara majhahns (rituals).

The Magical Caste System

Dehara follows the Wraeththu magical caste system. Caste in this case does not apply to rigid social status, but nine levels of three tiers through which the student, or rehuna, progresses. The nine levels are crowned by a level beyond corporeal existence, equating with Aghama, or divinity.

To pronounce these names, stress the syllables typed in bold.

KAIMANA (**Ky**-ee-**mar**-nah) 'The Path of the Seeker'

1: Ara - altar (**Ar**-ah)
2: Neoma - new moon (Nee-**oh**-mah)
3: Brynie – strong (**Bry**-nee)

ULANI (Oo-**lar**-nee) 'The Path to the Cosmos'

1: Acantha - thorny (A-**canth**-uh)
2: Pyralis – fire (py-**ral**-iss)
3: Algoma - valley of flowers (al-**goh**-mah)

NAHIR-NURI (Na-**heer Noo**-ree) 'The Path of the Infinite'

1: Efrata – distinguished (Eff-**rah**-tuh)
2: Aislinn - vision (**Ayz**-linn)
3: Cleatha - glory (Clee-**ah**-thuh)

Rehunas of Kaimana and Ulani are known by their level, i.e., an individual of Acantha level would be known as Acanthalid.

Ara – aralid
Neoma – neomalid
Brynie – brynilid

Acantha – acanthalid
Pyralis – Pyralisit
Algoma – algomalid

Once Nahir-Nuri has been achieved, however, the caste divisions are no longer used as a title of address. Rehunas of that caste are simply called Nahir-Nuri.

Majhahn Tools

The implement used during invocations and to direct energy during majhahn is referred to as the vakei. In the absence of this tool, the practitioner uses the first two fingers of their dominant hand to direct energy.

For some of the workings, practitioners can use shayyai, which are flame proof bowls of methylated spirits set alight. Other substances can be burned, such as ghee (clarified butter), in which case a wick will also be required.

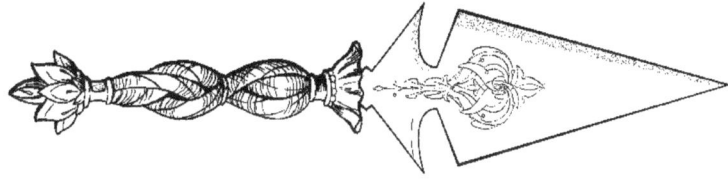

Symbols and Sigils

In Ulani, there are three symbols associated with the different levels: Acantha, Pyralis and Algoma. They have been 'programmed', (through the will and intention of those developing this system), to control energy invoked or created during the workings.

There are also different symbols for each dehar, for certain etheric locations, as well as for various aspects of the dehara. All of the symbols and sigils in the grimoire and its predecessor, *Grimoire Dehara: Kaimana*, were received during meditations.

Agmara Energy

All matter is made up of energy. At the microcosmic level, objects do not exist in the same way they are perceived by human senses. If people had the ability to perceive the particles of which things are made up, rather than just the human wider view of solid objects, it might be difficult to discern the boundaries between 'things'. In essence, all things would be linked, blending into one another. Energy is life. It is creation itself. It is what things are made of and is also the 'glue' that holds them together.

Practitioners of magic have access to this energy as a continual and limitless power source for their workings. It can help affect changes in the environment or be used for self-development. It is healing and promotes self-awareness.

Humans are part of this force, forever connected to it, born from it, returned to it. Whether we retain any form of consciousness beyond physical earthly incarnation is a subject that only the individual can make their minds up about, since there is no hard evidence about it. But few would argue that once we die, the energy of our physical form doesn't (indeed can't) just disappear. Energy can only change form, absorbed back into the source. This boundless fount of energy is referred to as 'agmara' in the Dehara system. The name derives from the Wraeththu progenitor and demi-god Aghama. It is the primary power source.

Appendix 2:
Majhahns of Ascension

By the time a rehuna reaches the caste of Algoma and becomes a hienama, they should have at least a basic ability to design majhahns for any situation or life event. This includes performing ascension majhahns, even though the true ascension of a rehuna takes place within the individual. Formal majhahns to mark ascension can be regarded merely as an enjoyable dressing, but are nonetheless useful and beneficial should rehunas be working together as a formal group, known as a ruhahn. For ruhahns, shared rites of passage can have more significance and certainly helps cement their mutual bond.

The core of an ascension majhahn performed on a rehuna by a hienama is attunement to the caste symbol. All other components can be designed to suit the individual or the occasion, and can incorporate aspects that are personal to the rehuna being attuned and to the particular caste being attained. Therefore, as part of the preparation, a discussion between hienama and rehuna should always take place to decide upon the details of the ascension majhahn, including how the Nayati or ritual space should be decorated, what music is included and so on. The rehuna may include poetry or other readings, as well as ritual actions personal to them, such as the creation of a commemorative talisman, if they so wish. Guests may bring gifts for the rehuna. Creativity and inventiveness should be encouraged to make the occasion as personal and meaningful as possible.

Basic Format of Ascension Majhahn

Preparation of location and participants (the hienama, the rehuna and if applicable other group members).

Invocation of relevant dehara or other entities.

Evocation of the particular caste correspondences to enhance the atmosphere, such as aspects of fire for Pyralis, flowers for Algoma and so on.

Other actions deemed appropriate to create sacred space or requested by the rehuna.

Declaration by the rehuna that it is their will and intention to raise their caste level.

Hienama calls upon agmara energy to empower the majhahn.

Hienama transfers the appropriate symbol into the rehuna either through breath, gaze or hands, or a combination of these methods.
    Breath – the hienama draws the symbol over each sikra of the rehuna's body and then uses the Breath of Lusteration technique. Build up the power of the breath and exhale over each sikra of the rehuna's body, 'sealing in' the symbol and empowering it.
    Gaze – the hienama draws the symbol over each sikra of the rehuna's body and then empowers it by 'gazing' agmara energy into the sikras. Agmara is visualised as streaming from the hienama's eyes.
    Touch – the hienama draws the symbol over each sikra and empowers it by placing the hands over the sikra, streaming agmara energy from them.

Visualisation or meditation decided upon before the majhahn – a visit to the Dehara Vegrandis in their temples, or some other personalised pathworking.

Declaration by the hienama that the rehuna's caste has been raised.

A feast within the ritual space shared by all participants.

Formal conclusion of the majhahn followed by celebration.

Appendix 3: Further Tribes of Wraeththu

This appendix gives additional information for rehunas wishing to expand up their work of visiting the hienamas of the tribes. Within these tribes, with their distinct customs and practices, ideas may be found for constructing majhahns for specific purposes. There are many more tribes within the Wraeththu Mythos, found in the novels and stories. A few examples are given here.

Froia

The Froia (*froy*-ah) are a Megalithican tribe of the Astigi marshes, who occupy the floating town of Orense. Their archon is known as the Braga. They completely conceal their bodies in robes except for times of ritual aruna.

The Froia venerate the physical body as the earthly representation of the divine. Their concealment is regarded as a shrouding of sacred secrets. The marsh on which they live is steeped in subtle energies; many different kinds of etheric forms dwell among the reeds.

A Hienama of the tribe would take a rehuna deep into the marsh in order to speak with them, and perhaps also to show them some of the bizarre wonders of the area.

Olopade

An isolated tribe northeast of Almagabra, the Olopade (*Oll-*

oh-pard) can be visualised as resembling an idealised, agricultural society. They are intimately connected to the land they inhabit, and its seasons. Unlike the Sulh, who share these traits, they are not overly mystical. Their magic is more of the folkloric kind, based in practical everyday life. They do not indulge in grand rituals, other than seasonal festivals, but are more aligned to working with herbs and charms.

The Hienama of this tribe can show a rehuna how to be alert to signs and omens in the world around them, and to learn from the behaviour of animals, birds and insects. He would favour the use of rhymes as magical words of power to be uttered over any charms he makes.

Parasiel

A tribe formed from the Varrs after the downfall of Ponclast. Now closely tied to the Gelaming of Immanion. The Parsics, of the tribe of Parasiel (par-*ah*-see-ell), are similar to the Olopade in many respects, except that they are far more intimately involved with the Wraeththu world and its politics. They can be seen as the ruling tribe of Megalithica. They also know they have a darker history, in that they evolved from the warlike Varrs, and for the older generation, this is never far from their minds.

But like the Olopade, the Parsics have great faith in folkloric magic, and the genius loci of local sites around them. Their Hienama is more interested in the restorative effects of his tribe's lifestyle and world view than a Hienama of the Olopade would be. The Parsics had a lot more to heal when power came to them.

Nezreka

An isolated forest tribe in Anakhai (a country west of Jaddayoth) whose totem is the wolf.

Visualisations to visit the Hienama of the Nezreka (nez-*rek*-ah) could involve the whole concept of 'running wild' with the wolf pack. A suggestion for this is to visualise a meeting with the Hienama in a forest. Sit down with him by a fire, and stare into his eyes, be drawn into his gaze, until you seem to pass through his eyes to a new landscape. Here you find the wolf pack, running through the wintry forest.

Freyhella

The Freyhella (fray-*hell*-ah) are a seafaring northern tribe of what was once Scandinavia. Very proud, they venerate harish versions of the Norse Gods.

The spiritual focus of the Freyhella is upon the sea and the winds – primarily because they rely upon these elemental forces for their livelihood. The Hienama of this tribe would also be adept at various forms of divination, not just with the derivatives of runes as used by the tribe, but by observing omens in the natural environment.

Teraghast

Teraghast (*teh*-rah-gast) consists of former Varrs exiled in the Forest of Gebaddon, and those who were later born there. They are led by Ponclast.

The Varrs inevitably lead to the Teraghasts, the debased remnants of the former tribe. The Teraghasts were warped by the strange energies of Gebaddon, becoming almost like beasts. They did not shun magic as in their early days, but embraced it. This was without any concept of restraint or compassion. They drank greedily of the mind-twisting energies in their environment.

The Teraghasts represent what can go wrong in magical training, should a rehuna become estranged from the world around them and begin to view it with contempt. The Hienama of this tribe offers a caution; take care not to end up like me. For that perhaps is the tragedy of the Teraghast. While they are what they are, they are not without self-awareness, even if it is coupled with far too much vengefulness and bitterness.

Resources: Books

Creating Magical Entities, Taylor Ellwood
*Pop Culture Magick, Taylor Ellwood
*Pop Culture Magic 2.0, Taylor Ellwood
*The Enchantments of Flesh and Spirit, Storm Constantine
*The Bewitchments of Love and Hate, Storm Constantine
*The Fulfilments of Fate and Desire, Storm Constantine
*The Wraiths of Will and Pleasure, Storm Constantine
*The Shades of Time and Memory, Storm Constantine
*The Ghosts of Blood and Innocence, Storm Constantine
*The Hienama, Storm Constantine
*Student of Kyme, Storm Constantine
*The Moonshawl, Storm Constantine
*Sekhem Heka, Storm Constantine

*Available as Immanion Press titles. See web site for details.
http://www.immanion-press.com

Glossary

Abrimel	A dehar demitto of Acantha
Acantha	The first level of the Ulani tier
Acanthalid	A rehuna of Acantha level
Aganymphna	A magical flower found in the etheric realms, with varieties having different properties
Agave	One of the major dehara, associated with fire, intention, healing, protection and aggression
Aghama	the dehar associated with the centre of a Nayati, spirit
Agmara	The life-giving energy of the universe
Aislinn	A level of the Nahir Nuri tier
Algoma	Third level of the Ulani tier
Algomalid	A rehuna of Algoma level
Alik	Heart va-sikra of the body
Aloyt	The dehar of dreams
Aloytic	Pertaining to Aloyt or his realm
Aloytia	The realm of Aloyt
Ara	First level of the Kaimana tier
Aralid	A rehuna of Ara level
Arehar	Alchemical dehar of calcination
Arojhahn	A seasonal festival
Arotahar	The cycle of the seasons
Aruhani	major dehar, associated with aruna (sex), life and death. Both creator and destroyer.
Aruna	Sexual activity between two hara
Astale	A term used to invoke dehara
Astraclaustri	A Constellatus, Gatekeeper of the Cosmos
Auracas	The elemental palace of Fire
Aurago	A spiritual guide of the Ulani tier
Aurith	Sacral va-sikra of the body
Avatar of Beauty	An epithet of the Aghama
Azul	Throat va-sikra of the body

Baloor	Alchemical dehar of distillation
Beautiful One, The	An epithet of Aruhani
Blue Flame	An epithet of Lunil
Brynie	Third level of the Kaimana tier
Brynielid	A rehuna of Brynie level
Chamber of Gateways	A visualised portal to imaginary realms
Cleatha	A level of the Nahir Nuri tier
Colurastes	An early Wraeththu tribe with a close affinity to serpents
Constellati	Beings of the ethers, avatars of the intelligence of the universe, sing. constellatus
Dark Hostling, The	An epithet of Ponclast
Dark One	An epithet of Aruhani
Dehar	An androgynous deity of the Deharan system of magic, pl dehara
Dehar of Aruna, Life and Death	An epithet of Aruhani
Dehar of Azure Light	An epithet of Lunil
Dehar of Dreams	An epithet of Aloyt
Dehar of Initiation, Knowledge & Inspiration	An epithet of Miyacala
Dehar of Silver Light and Initiation	An epithet of Lunil An epithet of Miyacala
Dehar of the Moon and of Magic	An epithet of Lunil
Dehar of the Mysteries of Aruna, Life and Death	An epithet of Aruhani
Dehar of the Mysteries of the Moon and of Magic	An epithet of Lunil
Dehar of the Sacred Fire	An epithet of Agave
Dehar of Ultimate Potential	An epithet of Miyacala
Dehara	Plural form of dehar
Dehara Demitto	Dehara created by the rehuna for temporary magical purposes
Dehara Vegrandis	Permanent dehara, lower in status than the 5 major dehara
Deharling	A young dehar
Devourer	An epithet of Aruhani
Divozenky	The personification of the earth
Dryalimah	The dehara term for the Tree of Life
Dvelin	Alchemical dehar of fermentation
Eburniel	A dehar associated with Rosatide

219

Efrata	A level of the Nahir Nuri tier
Elolis	Alchemical dehar of dissolution
Eviya	The area on the body, behind the navel, where the rehuna visualises their life force residing
Fayganza	Elemental Palace of Water
Forest of Ijhimere	Mythical location of Oorn, the Palace of Earth
Gelaming	A founding tribe of Wraeththu
Grissecon	aruna magic
Guardian of the Inner Ways	An epithet of Lunil
Guide to the Ways Below	An epithet of Abrimel
Halo of Agmara	A visualised circle of protective energy
Halo of Power	A visualised circle of protective energy
Har (hara)	Imaginary androgynous beings, intrinsic to the world of dehara.
Harhune	A rite of initiation, whereby a rehuna visualises acquiring a ritual androgynous form
Harrahn	A dehar demitto of Algoma associated with restfulness
He and She in One	An epithet of Agave
He Whose Body is the Sky	An epithet of Aruhani
Helek Sah	Underground city of the Krim Sri
Hienama	A magical teacher, created and visualised by a rehuna
Hienama of the Spheres	An epithet of Lunil
Hostling	A har or dehar who carries a pearl and gives birth to it
Hostling of Bones	An epithet of Aruhani
Igniteran	The etheric Nayati of Agave
Ignizil	A form of agmara energy associated with Lunil
Iskara	Third eye va-sikra of the body
Ivlizaar	Third eye sikra of the body
Iythra	solar plexus sikra of the body
Julangis	The etheric Nayati of Aruhani
Kaimana	The first tier of the Dehara magical caste system
Kakkahaar	An early tribe of Wraeththu associated with dark magic
Krim Sri	A race that predates humanity, guarding the mind of the world

220

Llah	Alchemical dehar of separation
Loraylah	The etheric Nayati of Lunil
Lord of the Cosmos	An epithet of the Aghama
Lord of the Libraries of the Cosmos	An epithet for Miyacala
Lunil	One of the major dehara, associated with magic, intuition, and the moon
Magari	A short magical working, a spell
Mahallatu, The	dehara demitto of Pyralis, 12 riders of truth and justice
Mair Vayairh the Golden-Eyed	A dehar demitto of Algoma
Majhahn	A magical ritual
Mal	Base va-sikra of the body
Malith	Crown va-sikra of the body
Merim	Leader of the Mahallatu
Miyacala	One of the major dehara, associated with initiation, knowledge and inspiration
Nahir Nuri	The third tier of the Dehara magical caste system
Nayati	A temple or ritual space
Nevaath	The base sikra of the body
Neoma	Second level in Kaimana
Neomalid	A rehuna of Neoma level
Nezreka	A Wraeththu tribe of Anakhai
Nimbara	Crown sikra of the body
Nyasava	Heart sikra of the body
Oorn	The elemental Palace of Earth
Otherlanes, The	Visualised pathways between etheric realms
Ouana-lim	The masculine generative organs of a har
Phynayel	Brother of the Mahallatu, dehar of healing, love, compassion and redemption.
Phynix	Alchemical dehar of coagulation
Ponclast	A dehar demitto of Pyralis, associated with Xephelax
Protector, Warrior & Healer	An epithet of Agave
Pyralis	The second level of the Ulani tier
Pyralisit	A rehuna of Pyralis level
Raatha	Throat sikra of the body
Rehuna	The term for any person working with Dehara

221

Ruhahn	The term for a group of rehunas working together
Ruuvaen	Sacral sikra of the body
Saal	Solar plexus va-sikra of the body
Samuntala	Etheric Nayati of the Aghama
Sarock	A founding tribe of Wraeththu
Sedu	A visualised creature that can
Sentinel of the Ways Below	An epithet of Abrimel
Shadowpeak	A mythical mountain at the heart of the world, location of Shuraya
Sharing Breath	An act between hara or dehara whereby information, images and feelings are transmitted intimately through the breath.
Shayyai	Burning lamps used for majhahn
Shuraya	The elemental palace of Air
Sikaara	The energy system of the body
Sikra	An energy centre of the body
Soume-lam	Feminine generative organs of a har
Sulh	A mystical, early tribe of Wraeththu
Tahanica	The Etheric Nayati of Miyacala
Thiede	A name for the Aghama when he appears in harish form
Tigron of the Spheres	An epithet of the Aghama
Uigenna	A primitive early tribe of Wraeththu
Ulani	The second tier of the Dehara magical caste system
Unneah	An early tribe of Wraeththu
Va-Sikra	Reverse or dark version of a sikra
Vakei	A ritual blade used in majhahn
Varrs, The	An early, warlike tribe of Wraeththu
Voorhalis	Alchemical dehar of conjunction
Walker of Battlefields	An epithet of Agave
Walker Upon the North Star Road	An epithet of Miyacala
Walkers Between the Stars	An epithet of the Constellati
Warrior of Eternal Fire, The	An epithet of Agave
Wraeththu	A fictional race of androgynous beings
Xephelax	The deharan underworld
Xynlis the Gatekeeper	A dehar demitto of transition, portals, and journeys

Also From Immanion Press

The First Volume of the Grimoire Dehara Series

Taking pop culture magic to a fine focus, this book is an introduction not only to the pantheon of this system, the Dehara themselves, but also to a new take on Neopagan practices, which involves the exploration of the androgynous nature of the soul.

This book is an essential addition to the library of any experimental practitioners of magic looking for something new to explore, as well as fans of Storm Constantine's work, who are interested in the background to the magic of the novels. ISBN: 978-1-905713-55-4. Price: £10.99 $19.99

Nayati Dehara
Etheric Ruhahn
www.NayatiDehara.com

Nayati Dehara was founded in 2011 as a working group to study and build upon the magical system first presented within *Grimoire Dehara: Kaimana*. Through group discussions, etheric rituals and daily meditations, a small, tight-knit group of Rehunas was created, dedicated to exploring and expanding upon the Deharan Tradition.

Today, Nayati Dehara exists as a gathering point for interested practitioners of any level, from the curious wanderer to the adept Rehuna, who seeks to explore aspects of Wraeththu spirituality, based on the pop culture magic system created within the Wraeththu novels, and paired with personal gnosis.

Within our forums, members share their experiences of the Dehara, trade tips and traditions, and work together in etheric exploration, with the aim to build community amongst those who are drawn to the Deharan Tradition and to help it grow.

So come, walk with us on the path that leads between the stars.

Hienama Mordraed har Sulh

www.NayatiDehara.com

Lightning Source UK Ltd.
Milton Keynes UK
UKHW040755120320
360231UK00003B/408